It's not where you start...
It's Where You Finish
THE STORY OF CAMBRIDGE COLLEGE

Celebrating a Cambridge College commencement.

3/31/22

Dear Julie,
Thanks for the part you played in this saga.
Love,
Eileen

It's not where you start . . .
It's Where You Finish

THE STORY OF CAMBRIDGE COLLEGE

Eileen Moran Brown

TIDEPOOL PRESS
Cambridge, Massachusetts

Copyright © 2022 by Eileen Moran Brown
Published in the United States in 2022 by TidePool Press

All rights reserved.
No part of this book may be reproduced in any manner whatsoever without written permission.

TidePool Press, LLC
6 Maple Avenue, Cambridge, Massachusetts 02139
www.tidepoolpress.com

Printed in the United States

Library of Congress Cataloging-in-Publication Data

Brown, Eileen Moran, 1937–
    It's Not Where You Start, It's Where You Finish: The Story of Cambridge College
    p.cm.
    978-1-7367720-0-3
    1. Brown, Eileen Moran 2. Education—Cambridge College
    3. Cambridge—United States—Biography 4. Social entrepreneurship
    I. Title.

2021951076

TO MY THOUSANDS OF STUDENTS
WHO TAUGHT ME MORE THAN I EVER TAUGHT THEM

*"How do you wake up one morning and
decide to start a College?"*

I am asked this a lot; and each and every time, I am thrown by the question. I can't imagine how someone could do that—or would do that. And that is not how it happened ...

—Eileen Moran Brown

Preface

On my first day as a teacher in a public high school in Philadelphia in 1959, one of my students, a young Black man, approached me to share some troubling news. He had just learned that the school had made a clerical mistake in assigning him to an advanced class the previous semester and was now preventing him from graduating because he had taken the courses out of order.

He explained to me, "I was assigned to a 12B English class last year, and I passed, but I skipped 12A. Now I have to take 12A and then take 12B next semester, so I'm going to drop out. I have to go to work. I can't afford to stay an extra semester."

"Don't even consider dropping out," I told him, "It wasn't your mistake."

When I brought my student's ridiculous situation up with the woman in charge of the roster, she said nothing could be done about it. I was surprised by her stubbornness. I was only twenty-one at the time, just out of college and full of hope and idealism.

"What if your son came home from school today and told you that there was a mistake in his schedule and he couldn't graduate?" I pressed.

"What does this have to do with my son?" She gaped at me with a baffled gaze.

"This young man is someone's son. He has a mother he'll have to tell about this sad and foolish situation."

"How *dare* you compare this boy to my son?" She responded with fury.

I could see that she was resolutely unwilling, maybe even incapable, of considering these two young men as deserving of equal treatment. Her son, like her, was white. My student was Black. The lesson here was one that I would come to learn over and over again in my time teaching in public schools in Philadelphia. Students of color were "other," less than, and not entitled to the kind of respect and consideration that was afforded to the white students. The same kinds of respect and consideration that I, as a white woman, had known all my life.

Several days later, the chair of the English Department took me aside after observing me teach. He told me, "You are a good teacher, but you were born with a silver spoon in your mouth. You must be careful with these students; you must not give them a glimpse of a world they will never see or give them a false sense of hope for what their lives could be like."

I was stunned by his words.

"It is *my job* to show my students that world, to help them to understand it is their world too, and to support them in learning the skills they need to be successful in that world," I told him.

He smirked at me and said, "You will learn that what you are trying to do is impossible." This was far from the last time that I would encounter such a sentiment.

I had entered teaching hoping that I could be part of creating the future of a more inclusive America. I wanted to be part of working toward the fulfillment of equal opportunity for all students. What I would learn, over the course of a long career in secondary and higher education, was how big a stake there was, and still is, in perpetuating the notion of two Americas—the idea that some people deserve opportunity and others don't.

I have spent a lifetime fighting that notion. It was the reason I joined with others to create Cambridge College—an institution of higher education created to serve a diverse population of working adults for whom those opportunities may have been limited or denied. Cambridge College was the culmination of many lifetimes of risks and choices, those of the people who worked with me and those of the people who came before us.

This book is about education. In a broad sense, it is about the American educational system and the story of how a new college was dreamed up and founded. But it is also a book about my own personal experiences and education as a white woman working for racial justice and equality during a time full of massive social changes.

The values that have motivated and sustained me in these efforts were shaped by the courage of my grandparents and parents to stand up for social justice and fair play throughout their lives, and by my childhood in small-town post-World War II America. I came of age during the quarter of a century following the War as the foundations on which our society had stood began to shift. The existing hierarchies of class, race, gender, and ethnic origins in the United States began to be challenged, and the profound injustice of racial discrimination began to be addressed. New and amended Civil Rights legislation, such as the Voting Rights Act of 1965, forced America's institutions to begin to change. The Supreme Court decided in *Brown v. Board of Education* (1954) that separate was not equal and that the public schools had to be integrated with all deliberate speed. And the end of the war in Vietnam as a result of public outcry marked a rare time that the American people themselves forced the government to change its foreign policy (at least as it pertained to Southeast Asia), and the *Roe v. Wade* decision gave women the right to choose what happened to their own bodies.

Although those years were filled with tremendous struggle, turmoil, and setbacks, there was a sense, at least in my mind, that the foundation had been laid for the country to become a level playing field out of which a true meritocracy could have grown.

It was a period of learning and of hope for many like myself who believed that the present and the future could be made better, that we could be the agents of that change, and that the general arc of our history as a country was one curving towards the good, that, as Dr. Martin Luther King often said during the height of the Civil Rights struggle: "The moral arc of the universe is long, but it bends towards justice."

Looking back on this all today, in 2021, that kind of hope feels far away. I have trouble looking at the current state of the world and feeling the same kind of hope that I felt setting out as a teacher in the 1960s—and that I continued to feel throughout my journey in creating Cambridge College.

It is true that we have made great strides as a country for racial and social justice, but there is still so much more that needs to be done.

The work must continue but the work requires hope. This is why I have written this book, because at its core this is a story about the power of hope.

So when people ask me how I decided to start a college, the answer is that the founding of Cambridge College was not the result of a sudden epiphany, and it was never a straightforward and linear progression. It was the product of the determination of many people to fulfill a mission. The belief that education—particularly higher education—must be for everyone, it cannot just be for the privileged and the lucky.

Chapter 1

I was born on November 7th, 1937, in Ashland, Pennsylvania, the heart of the Anthracite Coal Region when it was still thriving, and I was dealt a good hand to play.

My parents had just enough money in a small town to feel secure and to give me access to the modest social markers of my time: the Immaculate Heart Academy, the Fountain Springs Country Club, Camp Nik-O-Mahs, and Immaculata College.

At the time that I was born, the Irish were still considered second-class citizens, and I came of age as those ethnic barriers began to break down. The eventual election of John F. Kennedy to the presidency of the United States in 1961 had a profound effect on the way Irish people were perceived in America and the way they perceived themselves. As a child I was definitely aware of being Irish, but I felt proud of it, not limited by it. I never felt inferior and I had no need to feel superior, although I did feel very different from those around me.

As a teenager and young adult, I never thought in terms of a career. I just knew that there were lives I knew I didn't want—mainly any version of a life that was governed by other people's choices. I did not want to be, in the words of F. Scott Fitzgerald, "a hand moving among gleaming tea-cups, a voice calling to children."

My attitudes growing up were both a function of the era and the result of the circumstances of my childhood. The United States' entrance into World War II in 1941, and the changes that followed the War made an impact on the Anthracite Coal Region of

Pennsylvania where I grew up as well as on the country at large. The G.I. Bill opened up higher education to tens of thousands of returning servicemen, including my father, Francis. Various housing measures allowed many people to buy their own homes for the first time. And many of the women who had worked in offices, factories and munitions plants during the War had a new sense of their own possibility, including my mother, Mary, who went from working for a successful businessman to joining my father in starting a store.

I grew up different in a town where almost everyone tried to conform or was forced to conform. Everyone, it seemed, except my parents.

My mother's father spent his last years in a mental institution, and his breakdown meant that she had to give up her dream of going to college. Instead, Mary Morrisey went to business school and became an executive secretary/bookkeeper for a local businessman. She had learned from her own mother's life the importance of financial self-sufficiency.

I believe that my mother was determined not to be anyone's Irish maid, not even her own husband's or child's. She arranged to always have help in the house and rarely cooked. My father maintained that when they got married, my mother thought that an egg got softer the longer it boiled.

My mother thrived on work and had no inclination to be a mother. She went back to work right after I was born and hired a nursemaid, Mae, to take care of me. She talked about this all her life, regretting that it was true. Although her decisions caused me great pain as a child, I don't regret the choices she made and I came to realize as I got older that her life gave me the model and permission to do the same with my own. I grew up loving learning and being completely indifferent to all things domestic.

My father, too, was unconventional. Francis Moran, known to everyone except my mother as "Spike," was a force of nature—rugged, handsome, and smart. Even though he began his work life as a steamfitter, he read constantly, as his father had before him. He had a coherent world view that was vaguely Marxist and that informed everything that he did. Throughout his life, he acted on his own sense of social justice regardless of the consequences. He was once blackballed from a job because he led a wildcat strike when a co-worker was fired for getting sick at work.

During the War, he was riding on a bus one day back to his naval base in Norfolk, Virginia, where he was stationed, when a white man started to shout that a Black man was looking at his wife from the back of the bus. My father called out, "You silly son of a bitch, that man is minding his own business. He can't even see your wife from where he's sitting."

The bus driver stopped the bus and put both my father and the Black man off in the middle of nowhere. The man pleaded with my father to be quiet before he got the both of them killed. Then he took my father through the woods to a house where someone with a car could drive him to the naval base.

It was clear from stories like this that my father expected that I would live my life being true to myself and speaking up for what I believed in, much the same way he had.

On my first day in the first grade in the local Catholic school, St. Joseph's, I announced that I was not willing to die for Christ. Sister Devota called my parents and said, "Your daughter does not love Jesus Christ. She was the only student in the class who would not give up her life for Christ."

My father said, "My daughter is a child and she is not going to die for anyone. Stop asking her dumb questions and teach her something."

I learned two important life lessons from that experience. First, listen to your inner voice and don't pretend to be willing to do something if you are not. Second, there is a price to be paid for telling the truth. For the rest of my life in Catholic schools, I was the brazen little girl who was unwilling to die for Christ.

In a small town in a region of small towns, there are few secrets. You are judged, as Dr. Martin Luther King said in another context, by the content of your character. With my parents, especially my father, character trumped everything—money, status, race, religion, ethnic background, or any other possible classification.

In the world we lived in, the Roman Catholic clergy were completely above reproach, but even here my father applied his own standard of behavior. Our parish priest was a kind, generous man, who helped people in need whether they were Catholic or not. He did not adhere to the prevailing pieties of the time and my father admired and trusted him, even though he was very skeptical of the clergy in general.

My father used to say that you could always tell if a restaurant was expensive if there was a priest eating there, and he added that priests always seemed to have the prettiest "nieces" with them. Even back then, their dinner companions were more likely to be handsome "nephews," but my father, who I'm sure understood this, didn't point that out.

Though the clergy was a dominating presence in our lives, they were not the only influence in our small town. The town doctor, Dr. Robert Spencer, gained national notoriety by performing abortions in a clinic attached to his office. Believing that women should not have to go to back-alley practitioners, he had opened the clinic in the 1920s in order to offer women safer services, which at the time was illegal. A book was later written about Dr. Spencer called *The Angel of Ashland*. He took great risks for what he thought was right, and my parents, in keeping with their general unconventionality, respected him for that and supported him.

Many years later, in the early 60s, I was in Manhattan at El Morocco—a famous society nightclub of the time—and someone at our table asked where I was from. When I said, "a small town that you never heard of, Ashland, Pennsylvania." He said, "Ah, Dr. Spencer."

Ashland, along with rest of the Anthracite Coal Region of Pennsylvania in the 1940s, was the embodiment of Faulkner's line about life in a small Southern town, "The past is never dead; it's not even past." Each person carried his intergenerational history with him. My parents struggled to make their lives different, but they lived in the towns where they had been born and with the burdens of their history. The whole region lived under the long shadow of the Potato Famine, the Irish Diaspora, the Depression, and the War.

Coal mining was an integral part of our landscape and our lives. In the 1930s and 1940s, the mining industry was an almost feudal system of indentured workers. Most of the little towns were "patches," company towns built around a mine. The workers lived in company houses and bought their necessities at the company store. And most weeks ended with the workers owing more than they had earned.

Ashland, our town, was not a company town; it was where some of the mine owners lived along with the doctors, lawyers, and storekeepers. Nonetheless, on both sides of my family, there was a deep cynicism about wealth, authority, and hierarchy. Most of my relatives perceived the British, the Catholic Church, and the mine owners as exploiters of marginalized, hard-working people. When my parents eventually became successful business owners after the War, that same cynicism helped contribute to a feeling of constant tension between my immediate family and our other relatives.

Clinical depression traveled down the generations on both sides of my family. My maternal grandmother, Emily Broderick, got on the boat alone from Galway at the end of the 19th century at the age of fifteen to come to America. At home, her mother had read Shakespeare to the family in the evenings, but she had no chance for an education herself. When my grandmother wrote to American cousins asking if they would send her to school, they said "yes;" but when she arrived at their home in Philadelphia, they tried to turn her into their Irish maid. She burned every meal, broke every plate, and ripped every sheet until they gave up on that idea.

I don't know how my grandmother ended up in Gordon, a small town in the coal region of Pennsylvania. But it was there that she married my grandfather, William Morrisey, whose family owned a small hotel and tavern in nearby Ashland. These modest circumstances qualified the Morriseys as local gentry, and they did not approve of their son's marriage to an immigrant girl.

William and Emily married in spite of the disapproval of his family. William became the station agent for the Reading Railroad, and Emily began having children. During the birth of their first child, the doctor came directly from the house of a child dying of whooping cough and my grandparents' newborn became infected and died. My mother, Mary, was born next, and three more children followed. William's family never accepted his marriage to Emily, and though it is difficult to imagine how the families remained estranged throughout their lives in such small towns that were so close together, they did.

My grandfather William died before I was born. My sense is that he was smart, sensitive, and sickly. A lifetime of alcoholism made him angry and abusive. There was strong anti-Catholic feeling in their small town, and he was something of a firebrand. He campaigned for Al Smith, the first Catholic to run for president. In 1928, when Smith lost, William and Emily's house was stoned and all the windows broken. Shortly after this, William had a nervous breakdown. He spent the last three years of his life in a mental hospital, dying in 1934. This was a source of tremendous shame to his daughter Mary, my mother, and I was not told the mental hospital part of the story until I was in my early forties.

My grandmother Emily was made of much stronger stuff. In the early 1900s, four local members of the Ku Klux Klan came and burned a cross on my family's lawn. While four-year-old Mary and her three-year-old brother watched from the window, Emily went out and started to hit the Klansmen with a broom.

"You can hide your faces, but I recognize each of you from your big feet," she told them.

She called each by name and issued an order: "Clean up my yard and take the wood and gasoline to the Reading Railroad where you stole it or I will have you fired in the morning."

My mother said that she always remembered the sight of those men in their white outfits stomping out the fire and cleaning up the yard.

My grandmother was very entrepreneurial. Her little money-making ventures kept the family afloat after my grandfather's breakdown. She was very brave too—remembered best for nursing the dying during the influenza epidemic of 1918—and extremely literate. I didn't know until I went to school that the verses she told me at bedtime, by memory, were Wordsworth, Shakespeare, and Yeats.

But most of all, I remember my grandmother as deeply unhappy. Though she rarely talked about Ireland and never wanted to return, I don't believe she ever got over leaving her family at such a young age.

She was very bitter at my grandfather's family—at my grandfather himself. She was fond of saying, out of spite, that she had dropped an "s" from the spelling of the family name. This claim that she changed the family name was just one of her small acts of rebellion over her lifetime. There were few other ways for women of her generation to assert anger and power. She continued the family pattern, however, and disapproved of my father when my mother chose to marry him.

In the Moran family too, there is a history of intelligence, strength, and sometimes crippling vulnerability. My paternal grandfather, Martin Moran, was well-educated for his time and class. He became the youngest branch manager for the Metropolitan Life Insurance Company in Philadelphia. But he was so homesick for his family that he returned to Ashland and worked in the mines, for which he was ill-suited.

In Ashland, he became very active in union affairs. He was not a member of the Molly Maguires, the secret Irish union organization that employed violence against the mine owners to dramatize the injustices in their lives, but they certainly represented his point of view. He was also an alcoholic who did not suffer fools easily.

My paternal grandmother, Mary Agnes McKenna, was a strong-willed woman who had been quite happy before she married, working as a cook for a wealthy family in Philadelphia. But when her brother was killed in the mines, she had also returned to Ashland to be with her family, which was how she came to marry my grandfather in 1907.

I have always felt that my parents, the eldest siblings in each of their families, were haunted by this mix of shattered dreams, drama, and death. They carried the wounds that had traveled down the generations, but their will to thrive, not just survive, was stronger than their vulnerabilities. Both my parents were keenly aware of their immigrant roots and were determined to make better lives for themselves, for anyone who asked for their help, and certainly for me, their only child.

They lavished beautiful clothes and toys on me, in part to make up for their self-absorption and in part to defy their immigrant backgrounds. My mother's drive for respectability was fierce; my father's need for autonomy was foremost for him. They succeeded, but they paid a heavy emotional price. Their desire to make their lives different and better isolated them somewhat from their families.

When I was in the first grade, my mother had a rude awakening. From my bed one night, I called out "Mommy." When my mother came, I said, "I don't want you, I want Mae." My mother was so disturbed that she fired the nursemaid the next day.

Without Mae to take care of me, she sent me to an aunt's house after school to play with my cousins until she or my father picked me up. This kind of childcare was normal for the time, but the abrupt change was traumatic for me. I was a sad, shy, fearful, and awkward child, and I was hopeless at all the games that my cousins and their friends played. I had felt safe and comfortable with Mae, and now I was at the mercy of my cousins. Because of my clothes and toys, my cousins taunted me, saying that I was spoiled and that I believed I was better than they were. The truth was that I simply felt different from them and afraid of their taunts and roughhousing.

The next several years brought more upheaval and dislocation to my life. One evening when I was four years old, my family was having Sunday dinner after Mass at my grandmother Moran's house. The Longines Symphonette was playing on the radio, and an announcer interrupted the broadcast to say that the Japanese had just bombed Pearl Harbor. Someone asked, "What will happen now?" and my father said, "I don't know, but the world will never be the same." My father enlisted in the Navy shortly after that, and my mother moved to Norfolk, Virginia, to be near him.

During the War years, I lived apart from my parents even on vacations. In the summer during the War, my mother stayed in Norfolk with my father and sent me to her mother's and sister's family in New Jersey. My caretaking relatives felt I was too much like my father, too smart, willful, and different, and they set out to bring me down a peg or two.

My father Francis Moran, 1943.

My father and mother with me, 1945.

For second grade, my parents enrolled me in a Catholic boarding school far from Norfolk but close to Ashland—the Immaculate Heart Academy in Fountain Springs, Pennsylvania. I remember that it was always dark and cold there, and that all the nuns were crazy.

I found out years later that my childhood perceptions had been quite accurate. This private academy in the mountains was where, many thought, nuns with mental problems were sent there for a rest cure. Those nuns were our teachers. Today when friends suggest that I go to see plays such as *Nunsense* and *Sister Mary Elephant*—about how much "fun" nuns were in those days—I remember the petty cruelty of the nuns at the Immaculate Heart Academy and recoil.

The year after the War ended, my parents took the money they had saved from years of working, bought an empty building in Ashland, and started a small department store called Moran's. It would serve the town's professional people as well as the mining families in the surrounding towns.

My parents were both hard-working, creative, talented risk-takers—and great salespeople. When the War ended, everyone needed everything, and Moran's sold it: refrigerators, stoves, washing machines, toasters, coffee makers, irons, linens, rugs, lamps, and, at Christmas time, lots of toys.

My father had the ingenuity to start merchandise clubs. Once a week, he would go into the surrounding towns and collect a dollar from everyone who belonged to the club. This would give people a credit balance when they needed something, and every week there was a drawing with a prize of a $25 merchandise card.

This was a new idea for very poor people who lived week to week, and it helped create an additional customer base, along with the returning war veterans and thousands of others who had money and were starting families and becoming first-time homeowners in that crossover moment in American history.

Age 4, ready for Halloween.

Chapter 2

I was nine years old when we returned to Ashland, and with that return my days of being passed around to relatives and sent to boarding school were over. I attended fifth grade at the local Catholic school in Ashland, a stranger in my own world, trying desperately to hide my deepest feelings.

I never doubted that my parents loved me, but they were both self-absorbed and became increasingly consumed by the store. It provided them financial security, gave my mother the respectability she desired and my father his autonomy, but their devotion to the store made their nine-year old child feel even more abandoned, lonely, and lost. Yet I didn't want to upset them. They needed me to be a happy, uncomplaining child, and that was how I behaved. But I felt crippled by the sadness, anger, and fear that were frozen at the core of my being.

At ten, I started to develop excruciating headaches. That year, while trick or treating on Halloween, one of my cousins played a trick that humiliated me. I actually don't remember what the trick was, but I remember being so upset by it that I went home and begged my parents to move to another town. I also remember how baffled my parents were at such an extreme notion. The town, the store, and our extended families were their lives. They tried to reassure me as best they could.

The next day was All Saint's Day, and I had so much pain in my head that I fainted at Mass. My parents took me to an

Attending Immaculate Heart Academy in Fountain Springs, Pennsylvania, 1953.

ophthalmologist, who thought from his examination that I had a brain tumor.

It became clear later in my life that these headaches came from the deep emotional pain that I felt all the time in those days as a lost and, in some subtle way, abused child. However, no one, not even the doctors thought about psychological pain in those days. Exploratory brain surgery was scheduled a week later on my eleventh birthday, November 7, 1948, at the Jefferson Medical College in Philadelphia.

In the days before the operation, the clear message was that I was going to die during the procedure, although no one said this directly.

The day before, my parents were allowed to take me out of the hospital for what they thought would be my last meal. They told me to order all of my favorite things. My mother spent the whole meal in the bathroom throwing up, and my father tried not to get drunk. The next morning a priest gave me Extreme Unction, the last rites of the Catholic Church. Then they put me on a gurney and started to wheel me to the operating room but my father gripped the gurney.

He cried out, "I can't let her go. She is my whole life." They pulled him off and took me away.

When they opened up my head, they found I had a deformed optical nerve that had no pathological significance. But this diagnosis did not explain why I got such crippling headaches. Several days after the operation, the doctors suggested a frontal lobotomy to stop the pain of the headaches.

My father declared, "No, you are not doing anything else to this child." He came back that night and carried me out of the hospital against the doctors' advice.

My mother became distraught when my father brought me to the house in Philadelphia where they had been staying with friends during my operation. I can remember standing there frozen with terror while the children in the family stared at my shaved head, and my parents shouted at each other. The doctors scared my parents with their dire warnings that something was very wrong, though they couldn't say what exactly it was. Nevertheless, I did not return to the hospital.

My parents and I were so traumatized by the operation that the fear of further complications shadowed our lives for many years. For the rest of her life, my mother always said that any hope I had of a normal life was taken away when I was eleven years old.

I don't know what a normal life would have been, but I know that several themes related to the operation have dominated the rest of my life. The most profound of these was that I supposed to die but I didn't. This has often made me feel that I have been living outside the normal boundaries of time and space and has lent urgency to what I am doing in the present. I have often been aware of feeling, "For me, there is only now."

I have felt disconnected from the past and unable to imagine a future in which I would live the same life as the people around me. This disassociation has also led to certain recklessness in my personal choices, and a general disregard for thinking, "What will this mean for the rest of my life?" Only recently have I have begun to think there will be a "rest of my life," even though it seems a little late in the game for this line of reasoning.

After the operation, I returned to Ashland with an even deeper sense of being lost and feeling different from those around me. My near-death experience made me the object of fear and awe. I could feel that I made people anxious—and that I had cheated the town of a tragic ending.

The doctors cautioned my parents that after the strains of the surgery, a fall or blow to the head might kill me, so my parents treated me like a fragile doll. They felt guilty that they had neglected me, and they were consumed with fear that their neglect had caused my headaches. They never wanted me to ride a bike or roller skate, and I always felt that there was a bomb in my head that could explode at any moment.

My family and friends had no idea how to treat me, and the nuns at school seemed particularly irked by the whole situation. My parents had made a gift to the Propagation of the Faith in gratitude for my staying alive. The Propagation of the Faith purportedly "bought" "pagan babies" with these gifts, which in effect meant using the money to convert an African child to Catholicism.

The donor got to name the baby who would now have a chance to be a Catholic because of the "gift." As soon as I returned to school, the nuns gave me the honor of naming the baby that my parents' gift had "bought." The nuns suggested that I call her Eileen.

"No," I told them, "The parents have the right to name their own baby. I don't want to do this." Even though I had had my brush with death, I was still the heathen child who missed the point of Catholicism.

The following year, in the seventh grade, several themes of my life collided. One day in class, I nonchalantly passed a note for another student. The nun teaching the class saw and dragged me up to the front of the classroom and started to shout, "Roll out the red carpet. The Morans will be coming up. I'm beating their precious daughter."

She grabbed me by the shoulders and banged my head against the edge of the desk. I was too terrified to tell my parents, but my cousin Anne, who was in the class with me, told my Aunt Mary, who came to the house and told my parents. They became completely distraught. My father drove immediately to the rectory and told the priest that he was going to have the nun arrested for assault and battery. The priest promised my father that he would tell the nun that if she ever touched me again, he would go to the police with my father. After that, although she was my teacher for another year, she never bothered me again.

In the eighth grade, when the same nun told me to stand in the front of the line for the graduation procession, I pointed out to her that I was taller than some of the girls behind me and said that I thought everyone was being arranged by height.

"You have been brazen and questioning right to the end," she said as she glared at me. "You are first because you have the highest grades in the class."

She delivered this last line particularly scathingly, as intellectual achievement wasn't something the nuns admired, and especially not in me.

When I told my father some time later that I didn't believe in God, he said, "Don't tell your mother." In his eyes, I could do nothing wrong. My mother sent me to piano lessons and dancing school, and later on to tennis and golf lessons, but I was hopeless at everything. My father taught me to swim, and to this day it's the only thing I can do, other than read, talk, and think. But in those early years my parents had to live through the inevitable dance recitals, which my mother dreaded and my father loved. I was a stationary rose in "The Waltz of the Flowers." The dancing teacher's instructions to me were, "Don't move a muscle." My mother knew that it was not a good sign if you didn't get to dance a little at the dance recital.

With my father in Atlantic City, c. 1950.

My father was thrilled. He told everyone within earshot, "That's my daughter, the star, the rose."

I believe my father had a deep underlying despair that he fought with relentless optimism, a duality that I've shared with him throughout my life.

Among the influential events of my life were our Friday night football games. In the 1940s and 1950s, some of the country's best football players came from our region of Pennsylvania.

Many of the surrounding towns, especially those with coal mines, had powerhouse football teams. In those days, some of the high school players worked part-time in the mines and had the strength that only comes with such hard work. Since there was no mine in

Ashland, our town's teams were usually on the losing end. Still, every Friday night in football season, nearly every person in the town would walk to the stadium for home games.

For away games, my father took my mother, my friends, and me in our station wagon. Win or lose, it was serious business.

Usually, the opposing team would score quickly, and then kick the ball back to our team. My father always insisted that we stand for the kick-off. It was like clapping for Tinker Bell—the famous scene in Peter Pan where the protagonists try to restore the little fairy's vitality by openly proclaiming their belief in her. We had to make a show of believing that someone on our team would catch the ball this time and run the length of the field into the end zone.

Although I don't remember that actually ever happening, my father and I, undaunted, stood up every time. My mother refused to participate in this ritual; entirely too much getting up and down. Another idiosyncratic practice was that my father and I always shouted, "Go for it!" on fourth down, notwithstanding that it was usually "fourth and very long."

For the rest of my life I have "stood up for the kick-off" as I hoped that this was the time a student of mine or a dream would succeed, and would make it to the finish line.

My father was also quite a drinker. The prevailing view in the coal region in the first half of the twentieth century was that "drinking was a good man's fault." And "Spike" Moran was considered a good man and an even better drinking buddy.

But he didn't drink all the time and it never interfered with his managing the store. In fact, the only one troubled by my father's drinking was my mother, who carried the shame from her own father's life into our home. She fired a cleaning woman on the spot when she found her using the banister of our hallway spiral staircase to re-enact for me Daddy's having fallen from the second story balcony of a local bar the night before. My mother hated the Irish songs that dominated my childhood, while "Only Our Rivers Run Free" and the "Wild Colonial Boy" made my father weep. Worse yet to her was when he would render his own off-key version of "Galway Bay" or "Danny Boy."

My mother did soften over the years to the re-telling of everyone's favorite "Spike" Moran story. My father was celebrating St. Patrick's Day in 1956 (I was a freshman in college at the time) with some friends in a local bar when they met a young man who had just come from Ireland and was very homesick. My father went to the pay phone in the bar and called the young lad's Irish village. Everyone in the bar spoke to everyone there on the village's only phone. The next morning, my mother got a call from the telephone company to tell her that her son had charged a call to the home phone totaling $264.

"I don't have a son," my mother said. "That man is my husband."

In 1956, $264 was roughly a month's wages for a schoolteacher or a nurse and certainly much more than a miner made in a month. My parents, of course, paid the bill, and it remains an often-repeated story in the town.

A year or two after that famous phone call, I was in a bar in downtown Philadelphia with a man I was dating who said to the Irish bartender, "Doesn't Eileen have the map of Ireland on her face?" The bartender asked what county in Ireland I was from.

"Pay no attention to him," I said. "I'm from a little town in upstate Pennsylvania." "What town?"

"Ashland."

He then proceeded to tell me the story of my father, the homesick Irish lad, and the phone call. "I don't know how much it cost and I don't know the man's name, but it was such a splendid thing."

"It cost $264 and that man is my father." I told him.

But generous and affable as my father was, drunk or sober, my mother hated his drinking.

She felt that my father, who adored me, would stop drinking if I asked him to. I don't believe he could have stopped; it was his way of coping with the pain of the world. I never did ask him, and I'm sure that added to my mother's ambivalence towards me.

My whole world changed in high school. I returned to the Immaculate Heart Academy, this time as a day student, where I found my experiences as a student much better than they had been when I was younger. I also found myself part of a new community where people's interactions with me weren't colored by the aftermath of my operation. It was like the moment in *The Wonderful Wizard of Oz* when Dorothy's world goes from black-and-white to Technicolor.

My new peers regarded me as fun and interesting, and my teachers saw my intelligence as something to be encouraged. People also sometimes began telling me that I was "the most beautiful girl they had seen in real life," and that "women in magazines and in the movies were more beautiful," but that I "was real." I always felt like there were two ironic things about this. First, there was a part of me that never felt real; and second, as Rita Hayworth once said, her lovers went to bed with Gilda, a role she had played in a movie, and woke up, disappointed, with Rita Hayworth. Although I was too young for lovers in those earlier days, I felt that the boys that I dated then had an idealized picture of me that I couldn't live up to. This was often disorienting for me and disappointing for the men.

These were all such abrupt and unsettling changes that I felt lost in a new and different way, as though I were not quite the person that others had thought I was. A part of me remained the terrified child with the shaved head, but I could also feel that my own perspective of myself was starting to shift inside me.

I was first in my class at the Academy, and won a scholarship to Immaculata College, a small Catholic girl's school in suburban Philadelphia. My father had definite views about sharing what you had and not taking what you didn't need, and he felt he could afford to send me and left the scholarship for someone who needed it.

His views on money extended into other areas of my life. I never had a summer job, because he believed that jobs should go to people who had to make money for their families. Then there was tipping. He felt that if you could afford to stay in hotels, eat in restaurants, and ride in taxicabs, you could afford to be generous to the people who served you. To this day, I have several very wealthy friends who are mortified by how much I tip; they were brought up with the notion that it is vulgar and ostentatious to tip more than the normal percentage.

I saw people the way my father did. I never felt better than or less than anyone else. I have always been comfortable with wealthy, poor, and middle-income people, perhaps because of the unusual social structure of the coal region. I imagine it reinforced the notion that everyone is just who they are and should be judged on how they behave.

In the coal region, each town had a few people who basically owned the town, and everyone else worked for them, in the mines, or in other capacities. The children of these privileged people went to the Academy, belonged to the country club, went to nightclubs and dances, and did all the things that high school kids do together. Some of my friends in high school and college came from what constituted this "landed gentry" of the region. They were a small group of people, and the social stratification wasn't rigid. My parents were hard working and successful, but not wealthy and not of this class. Nonetheless, I was part of an inner circle, and no one questioned my right to be in it.

I didn't realize at the time what this inner circle meant for the people who weren't in it. A friend of mine from Ashland told me years later that he could still name every person in the town in the order of their place in the social hierarchy.

My friends who were at the top of this social hierarchy were big fish in small ponds and the deference that was shown to them and their families is shocking in retrospect but was very much taken for granted at the time. I can remember going into crowded clubs and having the owner ask people to get up from their table so that we could sit down.

One of the biggest fish was a friend of mine from Shenandoah. I was in two automobile accidents with him. One was serious. He was drunk and speeding and totaled his own car as well as the car he hit. Several people were injured, two very badly. When the police came, they handled it discreetly, with no consequences for my friend. That did not surprise me, but I did expect the local newspapers to cover it, since they even covered our birthday parties. My father told me that my friend's family would make sure there would be no record of that accident anywhere, and there wasn't.

Another occasion that stands out in my mind was my friend Marcia Murray's wedding, at which I was a bridesmaid. Marcia's family was very much part of the "landed gentry" of the region. As we were being driven from her house to the church, people came out and lined the street to see the wedding party. Seeing this, one of the other bridesmaids, a friend of hers from college, said, "Oh well, noblesse oblige," rolled down the window and gave a papal wave.

Years later, when my mother was in the regional hospital, her nurse said to me, "You were a bridesmaid in Marcia Murray's wedding, weren't you?" She then went on to say, "That's the last time my father left the house alive. He was very ill, but out of respect for the Murray family, he got dressed and stood on the sidewalk with the rest of the town to applaud as the wedding party passed by."

It is hard to convey now what a small, insular world ours was in those years, and the extent to which people knew one another. My parents were especially well known. Most everyone shopped at Moran's and belonged to our store's merchandise clubs. My mother was active in the small-town activities, president of charity drives, of ladies' committees at the church, and at the country club. My father was well known for his business and civic activities, and everyone had at least one great "Spike" Moran drinking story. Through all of this, I was "Spike" Moran's daughter, which meant that whether I'd met them or not, everyone knew me. And before I came down to breakfast in the morning, my father knew where I had been the night before and whether he approved.

It could be that my place in Ashland as a member of an inner circle prepared me for the surreal nature of so much of my life. But through all of those enjoyable and sometimes glamorous-feeling years as a teenager and young adult, I always felt that I was slightly disengaged from what was going on around me, as though I were playing a starring role in the movie of someone else's life.

Graduation from Immaculate Heart Academy, 1955.

Chapter 3

I majored in English at Immaculata College and became a student teacher at Haverford High School in a wealthy suburb on Philadelphia's Main Line. I loved teaching; one of my supervisors said that I took to it the way some people take to heroin. I connected with the students in a way that mattered to me and, I think, to them.

In 1958, in November of my senior year of college, some friends from Immaculata and I took the Philadelphia Teachers Exam, mostly out of curiosity. I was later pleasantly surprised to learn that I had that year's top score. Nevertheless, the possibility of my setting foot inside a classroom was remote. Like most women of my generation, I was encouraged to focus on preparing for marriage and motherhood, and this was the direction I assumed my life would take.

The following month, in December of 1958, I was introduced to a man considered one of Philadelphia's most eligible Catholic bachelors. Bill McGarvey was a successful stockbroker who had left the priesthood to go to the Harvard Business School. He told me once that he "felt he could do more for Christ in the world than in the priesthood." I was a possession he wanted, and he set about getting me. Instead of wondering, "What do I want for myself?" I went on playing my appointed role in the movie of the moment. That movie was *Beautiful Catholic Girl Has Been Chosen by Wealthy Catholic Man to be his Wife*. I was accustomed by then to being chosen, and I was strangely passive about it.

We began dating a month later, in January of 1959, and even from that point there were already troubling and off-putting things about Bill. Almost from the beginning, he worried that I might not be his "spiritual equal." Nevertheless, he tried to convince me to leave college and begin planning a June wedding for that same year. I was aware enough to say I didn't want to get married immediately and was not going to leave college before I graduated, especially since I was in my final semester and would be graduating that June. He saw no need for me to have a degree. As his wife, I would never work. And although he never said it out loud, he thought I was entirely too smart to begin with.

We spent a lot of time with other Catholic brokers and their wives. The men were knowledgeable about companies, numbers, and stock prices, and they discussed them endlessly.

I often spent those evenings talking to a piano player or a bartender. One night, we ran into a Jewish friend of mine from the University of Pennsylvania. After we left, Bill told me that he had to work with "Hebrew people," but he did not expect his wife to socialize with them.

"What a hateful thing to say!" I said to him in horror. I reminded him that as a Catholic, he had to know that "Everyone is made in the image and likeness of God" and that prejudice was a sin. I was shaken and revolted by his bigotry, but I did not have the insight to understand what it would mean for our marriage.

Despite my adamant declarations that I did not want to get married immediately, Bill gave me an engagement ring while we were visiting my parents over Easter vacation in April. He still wanted to get married in June; I insisted on waiting until August—after I had graduated.

We were both virgins, and Bill felt that because we were now engaged, we could have sex.

And so we did, such as it was. Incredibly, from that time on, he became consumed with the question of whether he should marry a girl who was not a virgin. Nonetheless the marriage plans continued: the engagement party, the notices in the Philadelphia newspapers and *The New York Times*, the invitations, the gifts.

I drifted through it all, playing my part. I remember reading bridal magazines and underlining the relevant passages; choosing sterling, china, and crystal patterns; going to endless "surprise" bridal showers hosted by my bridesmaids-to-be and various members of our families.

The 1950s were a pre-conscious time for me, and I think for most women my age. I didn't wonder how I could marry a man with such a shocking set of social values, a man who discriminated against people different from himself and who was so condescending toward me. My friends weren't crazy about him; but that wasn't really the point. Bill was an eligible Catholic man and he had chosen me. That was the point.

My father didn't like Bill, either. But his over arching concern was that I would be well taken care of. Even my mother was put off by Bill's insistence on praying before meals in restaurants and at the country club. She was hurt that he complained when she served a large meal during Lent, a time of penance.

Bill came to my graduation from Immaculata, in suburban Philadelphia. Afterward, I drove home to Ashland with my parents, and Bill intended to come up the following weekend. I lay in bed the morning after my graduation and saw the rest of my life scrolling out in front of me. The inner voice that had said, "I don't want to die for Christ" now said, "I don't want to marry Bill McGarvey. I don't want to be his possession for the rest of my life."

I knew that was how he saw me. I knew that he would never let me go if we got married, not because he loved me, but because he possessed me. Needless to say, divorce would be out of the question. I sat up and knew that he would have me committed to a fancy mental institution rather than suffer the disgrace and sin of divorce. I remembered that he had mentioned having twelve children, and when I'd said I would draw the line before twelve, he had said, "God will draw the line."

For the first time since I had met Bill, I took a realistic look at the rest of my life and knew that I could not go through with the wedding. In a state of panic, but with tremendous clarity, I picked up the telephone and called his office.

"He can't be disturbed," his secretary said.

"Get him to the phone," I said. "He will want to hear this." When I heard his voice a moment later, I said, "Bill, I don't think we should get married."

After a moment of silence, he said, "What do you mean? This has already been decided. You can't do this."

"Yes, I can."

I heard him sigh in exasperation.

"What made you come to this conclusion? Why now? What about all of the plans? What will we tell people?"

"I'll come to Philadelphia tomorrow. We can figure out what to do about all of these things, but I don't want to marry you. I don't think we would be happy."

"You are just being silly and immature. You just need to grow up."

What could I say to convince him? I came up with what I hoped would be the most compelling argument.

"I don't think I'm your spiritual equal."

I went on to catalog the many ways in which I believed I was inferior to him spiritually. "I don't pray every day. I don't worry constantly about sin. I don't avoid my unmarried friends who are living together. I know you think I am going to change and become more spiritual, but I'm not."

By the time he hung up, he understood that I was serious and the wedding was off. But what I remember most is my feeling that he didn't react as though he was losing the love of his life. He reacted as if his Mercedes-Benz had been totaled or his beach house had been flooded, and the insurance wouldn't cover the loss.

I went downstairs to break the news to my mother, who was as upset as I expected she would be. When I convinced her that I had made up my mind and that I had already told Bill on the telephone, she was horrified.

"The whole town probably knows this right now," she said, "and you haven't even told your father."

She was absolutely right. When my father arrived at the country club for lunch, a waitress said to him, "I hear Eileen broke her engagement."

I had jumped off a cliff, and there was no climbing back up. I realized that I had made a choice to blow up my life as I had known it. Now I was completely on my own to create the person I wanted to become. It seemed a small matter that I had no idea who that person was.

I took all that my life had taught me so far and all that I had learned from the lives of my parents and grandparents. I wasn't afraid to set out on my own; my grandmother Emily had come from Ireland by herself at fifteen. I trusted that I would figure out what to do as I went along. My parents had started a store in an empty building and were successful. They had made something large and wonderful from their own hard work and dedication. I didn't know exactly what I was meant to create, but I knew I was on my way.

Chapter 4

When I broke my engagement in June of 1959, I completely changed the pattern and direction of my life. I felt terrified and liberated, but most of all, I felt the freedom to make my own choices. I had the sense that for a little while my life was my own; that I'd won a reprieve.

I still assumed that someday I would get married and have children, but not yet. Beyond that, I had no particular ambitions, no urgent plans. I packed up a few things and went to stay at a friend's house while I assessed my options.

While I was staying with my friend, I received a postcard from the Philadelphia School District which informed me that my high score on the teacher's exam—the exam I had taken out of curiosity and without any real intention of ever going into the workforce—meant that I had qualified to begin working as a teacher in Philadelphia that fall. I decided that this was what I was going to do next: I was going to become a teacher.

To pass the time between June and the beginning of my new teaching position in the fall, I enrolled in a summer program at University of Pennsylvania. I had taken several courses in English literature at Penn during the summer between my junior and senior years at Immaculata College and had enjoyed being a student there. I felt that going to back to school for the summer would be a safe alternative to staying at home in the wake of breaking off the engagement. When the program started in July, I moved into a dormitory on campus.

At Penn I found myself a shell-shocked innocent adrift in a much more sophisticated world than I had ever known. Until then, I had lived in a predominantly Catholic universe—not a stuffy world for the most part, but parochial nonetheless. I knew what I didn't want, but I hadn't a clue about what I wanted. My engagement had been so unsatisfactory and so suffused with guilt that I spent the rest of that summer celibate. Even when I started to date and go to parties later in the summer I always returned alone to my dormitory room as though it were a convent.

Toward the end of that summer, I began preparing for my new job which meant, among other things, finding an apartment in Philadelphia. Two of my friends from Immaculata wanted to live with me, and I found us an apartment at the edge of the Penn campus in a complex called The Hamilton Court, which included a hotel as well as an apartment building.

Once we moved in, we learned that the whole complex was owned by the Philadelphia mob.

Sonny Liston, the heavyweight-boxing champion in 1959, lived in the Hamilton Court Hotel with luminaries of questionable reputation. The hotel bar, a cosmopolitan spot, was frequented by local mob hangers-on, college kids, neighborhood people, and businessmen staying in the more up-scale Sheraton Hotel across the street. Lil, the hostess, conducted business at the bar, including running a discreet call-girl operation. In the daytime, she was the cashier at the delicatessen next door.

I was not at all troubled by the characters at the Hamilton Court. To the contrary, I enjoyed the color and richness of my new surroundings. Having grown up in a small town, I was accustomed to responding to people by the way they treated me. I did not judge other people's lives, and I enjoyed the sense of not being judged in turn.

The apartment building was filled with its own mix of wealthy Wharton School students, mostly from Latin America, just-out-of-college kids like my roommates and me, some fairly shady but always pleasant men, and occasionally women, whose origins were unknown.

The postcard I had received earlier in the summer from the Philadelphia School District had instructed me to come in and pick the school where I wanted to teach, a privilege I had earned because I had the top score on the teacher's exam for English. On my visit to the Central Administration Building, I told the man in charge of assignments that I wanted to teach at the high school closest to Penn, the West Philadelphia High School. He looked at the directory of schools and then up at me.

"That's not possible." He said. "What's your second choice?"

It didn't occur to me at the time to ask why my first choice wasn't possible. I later realized that he didn't want to place me there because West Philly was almost entirely African-American. I looked at the directory and chose the next closest, the John Bartram High School.

I arrived at Bartram for the teacher's orientation the day after Labor Day 1959, wearing a pink linen suit with a hat and white gloves. Stepping into the central hallway, I felt happy to be starting my life as a teacher. Bartram High School was in a large, aging building in a white working-class neighborhood in Southwest Philadelphia. The demographics of the school echoed those of the neighborhood, about 65 percent of the students were white, the other 35 percent Black, and all of them from working-class families. I felt I was entering a different but parallel universe.

At twenty-one, I was the youngest teacher ever assigned to teach in Philadelphia's high school system. Most new teachers started in a junior high school; if they were lucky, they moved up to high school. I have no idea why they chose me to be the first one to skip this step, but then there were so many things that I had no idea about.

On the first day, there was a two-hour orientation for new teachers. It was a very pragmatic presentation. I wrote down every word and the next day did exactly what I had been told. One of the older teachers took me aside and gave me a list of words to avoid saying or writing on the blackboard. They were common words, including "come" and "blow," and I was completely mystified about why to avoid them, but I didn't ask.

The afternoon of that first day, I got my teaching assignments: five classes and a home room, which meant that I was the advisor for thirty kids. I was expected to take their attendance and handle bureaucratic details. Because I had gone to a small private academy, I had no experience with this concept, but by carefully following my hand-written "orientation" notes, I managed.

The most onerous record-keeping task was having to separate each and every category into Black and white students, including daily attendance. As time went on, invariably, I would write down the total number of students who were absent or late but when I had to hand in the tally, I would frantically try to remember the Black and white breakdown. I would take a guess and hope for the best.

At Bartram, the students were separated into six levels or tracks. Those in the top two tiers were "block-rostered," which meant they took all of their classes together with the best teachers. The "A" block was the best, and "B" block, second best. In my early years at Bartram, only white students were in those block classes.

The remaining students were divided into four tracks: The "X" level, the best of the rest; the "Y" level, the next best and the largest number of kids; the "Z" level, for "slow" kids; and what was called the "Modified" level for those students considered "non-educable," or, in the troubling parlance of the day, "orthogenically backward."

My five classes included tenth, eleventh, and twelfth grade English spread over four of the lower tiers: one "X", two "Y's", one "Z", and one "Modified." Each class had about thirty kids. I also had lunchroom duty with another teacher supervising 1,200 kids in a large cafeteria.

The orientation day with the faculty and staff was largely pleasant and informative. Because I was so young, the teachers treated me with curiosity and kindness. They seemed concerned that this inner-city high school might not be the right place for me, and they were dubious about my ability to succeed. I, on the other hand, was excited about the prospect of meeting the students the next day and beginning to teach.

But the next day brought more chaos and befuddlement than I had expected. My home room class turned out to be a group of seniors in their last semester. They included several students close to my age and a room full of savvy kids determined to make sure they graduated on time, whether or not they had earned that right.

As I called the roll and handed out their rosters, I automatically addressed the students as Miss or Mr. with their surname, without thinking about what I was doing. The respect, and though I didn't realize it at the time, the novelty, of my doing so had an instantly soothing effect on the room. It was immediately after this that the student whose story I told in the preface to this book (who was being prevented from graduating because of a clerical mistake on the part of the school), approached me with his problem. And it was not many days after this that I had a troubling conversation (also mentioned in the preface), with the department head in which he warned me against showing my students a glimpse of a world that he assumed they would never have access to.

These two experiences were mirrored in an interaction I had with the administrator in charge of evaluating new teachers, who also observed me in those first few weeks. After sitting in on one of my classes he came up to me and said, "Full many a flower is born to blush unseen, and waste its sweetness on the desert air."

I could see that he was smug and proud that he could quote from Thomas Gray's "Elegy Written in a Country Churchyard" off the top of his head. I was also aware that in effect he had managed to flirt with me and insult my students at the same time.

"I definitely do not see the students as desert air," I said to him, "I know that my teaching isn't wasted. These students are learning."

In each of these situations with the roster chairman, the department head, and the evaluation administrator, I said what was true for me, but beyond that I didn't know what else to do. The polite world that I came from had not prepared me for the hatefulness and

Teaching at Bartram, 1961.

bigotry I was now encountering at Bartram.

Over time, I came to learn that many of the teachers were first-generation college educated, and I saw how they contemptuously lorded this over the students who, a generation before, the teacher's own parents had been. The students knew that the teachers looked down on them. They knew that they weren't valued by the adults in the school, and for many of these kids they also knew that they weren't valued by their immediate world outside of the school as well.

I felt a sense of connection to those students. I had come to teaching in flight from the path that the outside world had chosen for me. And when I started to teach, I felt at home for the first time, felt that my whole self was completely accepted, that the students knew and understood the "pilgrim soul" in me. I felt a sense of exhilaration that I was doing something that mattered, and I felt a bond with the kids that I had never known anywhere else. And as I taught, I was very slowly coming into a fuller consciousness of myself and also of the country and the world in which I lived.

The joy I found in teaching was an incredible gift from the universe. I felt such a strong bond with my students and had such a clear perception of the tremendous potential within them that was overlooked by the larger society and by the school itself. I looked forward to each day despite the exhausting struggle of helping students catch up on all they had been denied—and despite my even more exhausting battles with bureaucracy.

The administration of John Bartram High School never understood the passion I brought to my work there. To those around me, I was the embodiment of 1950s American aspirations— an attractive young woman, well-educated, and financially secure, who had grown up cloistered and comfortable in a small town and now moved in sophisticated city circles. As time went by, I found that this image, like my high heels and white gloves, could be a useful camouflage.

When I wasn't teaching at Bartram, I was living my life against the zany backdrop of the Hamilton Court, and embracing the colorful environs I now found myself in. I dated unusual and exciting men: a Latin American oligarch, and an Italian prince, as well as more ordinary ones like the Philadelphia lawyer who figured out before I did that I did not really want to be a wife.

On the corner, next to the Hamilton Court, was a dry-cleaning business run by a man named Curley Jean. Early on, I dropped my dry cleaning at Curley Jean's. Whenever I tried to pick something up, Curley would say "Your clothes aren't back yet." I never thought to ask "back from where?" One Monday morning, I realized I had nothing to wear to school. I threw on a trench coat and ran down the fire escape to the store. "I don't have anything of yours back yet," Curley Jean said, "but I do have a couple of things that I've pictured you wearing." He brought out several dresses that clearly belonged to some of Lil's ladies of the evening. Only then did I realize that Curley Jean's was not actually a dry-cleaning establishment.

If someone was foolish enough to leave clothes, he sent them out to be cleaned, but it happened so infrequently that he didn't have a great system for getting them back.

I traipsed back up the fire escape, borrowed a dress from one of my roommates, and took a cab to school. When I told Lil that I didn't understand why Curly Jean pretended to be something he wasn't, she explained that he was a bookie with a gambling operation in the back room. The clothes on the hangers provided a front, and I was one of the only people who hadn't already figured it out.

I was getting a different kind of education at Bartram. My first act of rebellion came about inadvertently. During the first semester, I was in the teacher's lounge talking with Charlie Askew, who was the only African-American teacher at Bartram.

"I'm concerned about why we have to separate students into racial categories on all of the school's forms," he said.

"I wondered about that too." I told him. "Let's go ask the principal."

When we got in to see the principal, he gave us a cryptic answer. "We send the forms to the Central Office," he said.

"What do they do with them?" we asked.

"I don't know," he replied.

"Can someone from the Central Office come and explain it to us?" I asked.

The principal sighed in annoyance as he looked from Charlie to me and back to Charlie, perhaps hoping we would tell him we weren't serious about this bothersome question. "I'll look into it," he said, but it didn't sound as though he meant it.

Later in the day, the principal called me out of my classroom. "Miss Moran, you are very young and naïve," he said gently. "You don't want to get mixed up in this kind of thing. Before we know it, we are going to have to form a National Association for the Advancement of White People."

I was shocked. Charlie and I had just wanted the information. I hadn't thought that it was a political question. I didn't know what to say. I think I managed a bewildered, "Thank you." I never mentioned the incident to Charlie. I *was* naïve, but I was learning quickly and becoming more radical with every encounter I had.

No one from the Central Office came to explain the use of racial categories, but the atmosphere at the school was charged with race consciousness as the ongoing civil rights movement carried on in the country and in the city around us. Leaders from the local Black community got more involved in the school, and, in response, the white community surrounding the school building became more hostile.

Although I loved teaching, I didn't think that I would have the freedom to teach for the rest of my life. As a young woman in the early 1960s, I still felt I would have to get married at some point. But in the meantime, my life proceeded on two parallel tracks. I went to Bartram every weekday and stayed at the school until I had marked all my papers and prepared for the next day. Back at the Hamilton Court, evenings and weekends were filled with dates and parties with old friends, new friends, and the eccentric cast of characters from the complex.

Sonny Liston wandered through the bar, the delicatessen, and Curly Jean's. He liked to play practical jokes on unsuspecting people, but he did not like it when someone tried to trick him. A man I dated at the time had a recurring nightmare that he inadvertently annoyed Sonny and got beaten to death.

"Blinky" Palermo Jr., the son of the Philadelphia version of the Godfather, took quite a fancy to me and called with invitations to everything from dinner and dancing at a New Jersey nightclub to flying with him to Chicago for the Liston-Patterson fight in September 1962. Although I never went anywhere with him, he persevered with good humor.

I remember it all as a time of high spirits and good cheer. The whole building complex was connected through a system of house phones that worked both ways; it was possible to call the delicatessen at any time to get just about anything. None of us ever tested the limits of what "just about anything" meant, but I believe that if we had really needed something, Lil would have found it, if not at the deli, then at the bar or at Curly Jean's. It's hard to imagine what those two couldn't come up with. Lil was a great surrogate mother. She could diagnose minor medical problems, sew in an emergency, and give culinary advice. One of our friends called down one time and asked if they had any scruples. "Wait a minute," the guy said, "I'll ask Lil." He came back and said, "That ain't funny. Them's morals."

It was also a time of absolutely no fear. The apartment door wouldn't stay closed unless the dead bolt was on, and because no one ever remembered to take a key, we always left the door slightly open. Friends came and stayed with us. Occasionally we'd find some man that we didn't recognize sleeping on the living room sofa, but he would wake up and know someone who knew one of us and join in the revolving door of people who passed through our lives.

Wealthy Latin Americans attending the Wharton School or Penn Law School inhabited three apartments. It seemed that there was always a party in one of them. On Saturday nights, parties in all three would end up enveloping the whole complex with an amazing mix of people drinking, dancing, and spilling out into hallways, staircases, and courtyard.

Neither of my roommates worked. In fact, I may have been the only person in the entire Hamilton Court complex that got up every morning and went to an actual job. If I got up early enough, I could run two blocks, catch a bus, change to a trolley, and end up forty-five minutes later at Bartram. But that almost never happened. Instead I would cross the street to the Sheraton Hotel and get a cab. I was making the princely sum of $4,200 a year and was paid every two weeks. I would pay my cab fare the first week, borrow money from the doorman the second week and pay him back on payday.

Invariably the cab driver would ask a version of, "Why would a nice girl like you be going to a place like Bartram?"

To which I would reply, "If you want a tip, don't say another word."

During that first year, I dated a man named "Dutch" Shutler, who was finishing up at Wharton.

He had been the quarterback on his high school team in Wichita, Kansas, and won a football scholarship to Penn. He was handsome, fun, and very ambitious. He knew he was a long way from Wichita and was never going back. He always knew how he wanted his life to turn out, and he wanted me to be a part of it, but he figured out long before I did that I wouldn't be willing, or perhaps even able, to fill the role of corporate wife that the script of his life's movie required. He was accepted to Cornell Law School. I flew to Ithaca with him when he made the decision to enroll, and we continued to see each other for the rest of his time in Philadelphia.

He referred to the Latin Americans who lived in our building as "the Garchs," because of their reputation on the Penn campus as members of the oligarchy in the mostly Central American countries from which they came. My roommates and I grew friendly with them, and guided them through some of the oddities of American life.

On Halloween, Federico Blohm, from Venezuela and so wealthy that everyday life was beyond him, rapped frantically on our apartment door to say that there was a group of Black children in costumes at his door saying, "Trick or Treat."

"What do I do?" he asked.

"If you don't have candy, give them money."

I went to his apartment to find him handing out five- and ten-dollar bills to these overjoyed children.

When Dutch and I were together, we drifted through this scene together, even though he didn't particularly approve of my Latin American friends and their extravagances. We went to the racetrack once, and Federico insisted on betting on every horse in every race, defeating the purpose of the endeavor and creating a nightmare for me, the custodian of the betting slips. The Latins didn't much like Dutch either; he was so quintessentially the All-American guy. But it was very much a "live and let live" time.

When Dutch left for Cornell, I missed him. We wrote and talked on the phone and saw each other a few times, but he was on the search-for-a-suitable-wife track, and I didn't want to be anywhere near it.

Chapter 5

Even though I, as a white woman, was a part of mainstream America by virtue of the color of my skin, I had always felt profoundly like an outsider.

That feeling drew me to my inner-city students, many of whom had been abandoned by those around them. In my first days at Bartram, I felt like a visitor from another planet. But before long, I felt I fit right in with the students, and in my eight years there, I learned just about everything I know about teaching. The students from whom I learned the most were those in my "Modified" class during my first year at Bartram.

There was nothing subtle about the designation "Modified." And it was very telling that these classes were almost always entirely African-American. In the school's view these students were limited in a profound sense. They were the bottom of the barrel, and they knew it. Their rosters, their books, their very persons it seemed, were stamped "Modified." Although the faculty saw these students as an undifferentiated mass of slow learners, or as students with "behavioral issues," in my year with them, they taught me some of my most significant lessons. Not only were some of them among the brightest students I ever taught, but they were each insightful about one another's strengths and vulnerabilities, their possibilities and limitations for learning. And like all my students, they were infinitely resourceful in negotiating the culture of the school.

James was one of the most easy-going and gregarious students in this class. But one day early in the semester, he became belligerent and disruptive during a class reading exercise. I wasn't sure what had happened, and some of the students saw my surprise.

After class, I found a note on my desk: "James got mad because he doesn't want you to know he can't read."

The next day, after I talked with him and he had agreed to my proposition, the class and I embarked on a "teach James to read" project. I asked four students I knew were good readers to help me. James and I sat down with them, and we went over the fundamentals of reading together until James was able to "break the code," to begin to understand how to sound out words and attach meaning to them. We were able to do that in one period while the rest of the class did their homework. After that, James worked with one of the four students every day until he could begin to read on his own.

Several weeks later, James came up to me before class one day and said, "Miss Moran, I passed a sign that I have seen all of my life. I did what you taught me. I broke the word into parts and sounded it out. The word was 'railroad.' I was really proud."

"James, there have to have been teachers who tried to teach you to read before the tenth grade. Why did you choose to learn now?"

"Because it meant so much to you."

I tried not to cry. I was proud of James and also sad for him, that no one had cared enough to teach him to read. I knew too that there were many other students like James who would never get a chance to learn to read. Over the next several months, I assessed the learning levels of my students and saw that their ability level had almost nothing to do with the track to which they had been assigned.

But I never learned to gauge their level of psychic pain. Many of them had suffered wounds that were unimaginable to me, though not to their fellow students.

Ernest was another student in James' class. He had difficulty learning and would often become frustrated and angry. He was skillful with his hands for both good purposes and not so good. He frequently fought with other students, but if he could be helpful, he was always proud. In the metal-shop program, he would solder the handle back onto my handbag every time it broke off after I had stuffed it too full.

One morning, as I rushed to class, close to being late as usual, I found Robert, another student in the class, waiting for me outside the classroom.

"Miss Moran, something very bad must have happened to Ernest," he said urgently. "He is really angry, and I think he'll hurt somebody."

"I'll talk to him."

"I don't think that will be enough. He feels bad about himself, and he needs something to make him feel better about himself."

"I imagine you're right, but I don't know what that would be."

"Will you let me break the handle on your pocketbook?"

That's what he did. I walked into the classroom and asked Ernest to take it to the metal shop and fix it. And we all made it through another day.

This group of students also taught me the ways in which playing to a stereotype can be a way to work the system subversively. I had ordered "Good" books for my class instead of the dirty, disintegrating ones that were reserved for the "Modified" students. The class and I took pride in the completely intact books that didn't say "Modified," and I delayed facing up to the day when the head of the English department, who viewed the book-supply room as her personal library, would discover that I had no "Modified" books to return and more "Good" books than I had "Good" students. She kept careful track of these matters. I knew I would be discovered and duly reprimanded.

On Book Return Day I found that the extent of my culpability had widened considerably. In quite a few cases, the careful socialization of a decade of schooling had triumphed and many of my students had lost the "Good" books. But, as usual, when I had a problem, I asked the students for help. I shared my concern about returning fewer books in the wrong combinations with them. As usual, they had a solution. They told me to take up the cards with the names of the books on them without the number of returned books written in, and they would carry the books themselves.

We set forth. I was a nervous wreck; the students were delighted by the challenge. When we got to the book-supply room, four students dashed over and started putting "Good" books on the "Modified" shelves.

Mrs. Weiner, book-supply room major domo, immediately began screaming. "No, no, never put the books on the shelf until I count them. I can't trust your count. Take those books off the shelf."

At which point the students began frantically removing great quantities of books—both "Good" and "Modified." Once this removal process got underway to her satisfaction, Mrs. Weiner turned her scream on me. "You know better than to have the 'Modifieds' return books. Even you can see that they are too dumb to follow directions."

When this incredible scramble was over, the books were piled on the floor to be counted, and it turned out that I had returned more books in each category than I had received. This rare feat mollified Mrs. Weiner, who made a point of mentioning at the next department meeting that, at a time when teachers were losing books, "Miss Moran found extras."

When my fellow department members were duly impressed, Mrs. Weiner hastened to add, "But Miss Moran did a very foolish thing. She permitted the 'Modifieds' to carry up the books, and they could have ruined Book Return Day for her."

Over the course of that first year of teaching, I began to confront the injustice that I saw every day in a more aggressive way. I went from politely telling the truth to having angry encounters with anyone who behaved in an egregiously insulting way toward the students. I had to choose my battles, because nearly everyone who worked at Bartram was at least mildly insulting to the students.

Just as I had been "the brazen heathen child not willing to die for Christ" in my Catholic elementary school, I became the deluded

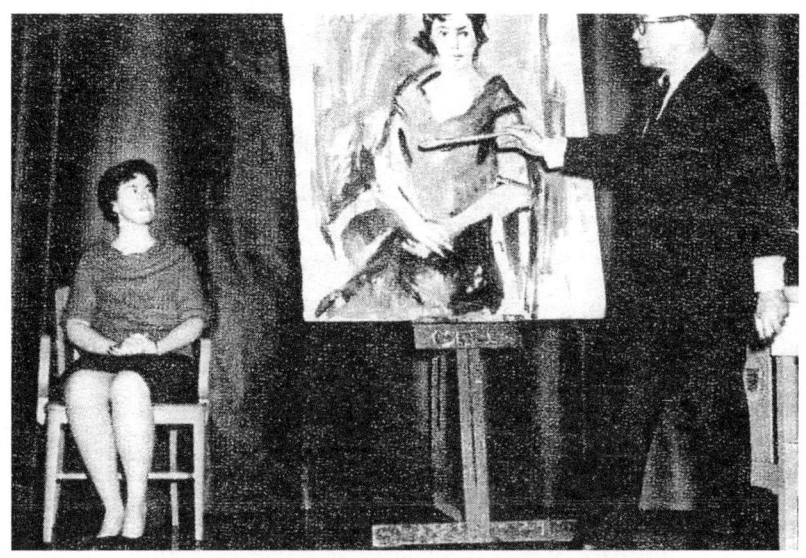

Sitting for a formal portrait at Bartram. A donor commissioned artist Doyla Goutman to put on a demonstration of portrait painting and students chose me as the subject.

radical white teacher who always "took the side of the kids" and didn't understand the importance of keeping things as they had always been.

The white teachers had a name for what they thought I was, and they often used this epithet behind my back and sometimes to my face. I think it was especially annoying to some of the teachers that, radical or not, I was also an upper-middle-class woman living a glamorous life that they occasionally read about on the society pages.

The high point of my incongruous social life was my relationship with José Miguel Bonetti, a student at Wharton from the Dominican Republic. We often went to New York City on weekends where his family kept an apartment in the Savoy Plaza Hotel, at 59th Street and Fifth Avenue. He was very careful about my reputation and always got me a private room. We would go to El Morocco or the Stork Club where he and his friends were well known, in part, for their generous tips. When someone asked if they were discriminated against, he said, "Money is always green."

José Miguel was very romantic. On my birthday he arranged for a Mariachi band to play on the fire escape of my apartment to wake me up. As I remember that year, it seems that there was always music playing. When we went out to dinner or to a nightclub in Philadelphia, he would often arrange for the orchestra to play our song, "An Affair to Remember," as we arrived.

There were always flowers, gifts, and special surprises. He knew that I loved the ballet and arranged for my roommates to go with us to New York to see the Royal Ballet with Margot Fonteyn, whom we went backstage to meet. José Miguel had met her on Aristotle Onassis's yacht after Grace Kelly's wedding. That was my favorite name-dropping sentence, but he was just explaining how he knew her.

Through all of this, I got up every morning and went to teach at Bartram. José Miguel sometimes went with me to school events, including the Senior Prom and the City Championship basketball game. Bartram played West Philly in a game that went into a sudden-death period after two overtimes, a first in high school basketball. Although Earl Monroe, who became one of the all-time great NBA players, was on the Bartram team, West Philly won in the third overtime.

If José Miguel and I were going out, he would send a car and driver to the school. The kids loved this and they would run to find me when the car came. On a Friday afternoon in early June 1961, it awaited me at the curb.

When I got in, José Miguel said, "El Jefe, Trujillo, is dead. I am going directly to New York to be with my parents."

I learned later that José's father insisted on returning to the Dominican Republic. "I stood with him in life," he said. I'll stand with him in death."

I always felt that there was a kind of gallantry in that. After José Miguel's father left for the Dominican Republic, Mrs. Bonetti, José Miguel and I had a bodyguard in New York, and in Philadelphia, until it became clear to the Bonetti family that the CIA had killed Trujillo. They weren't likely to move on to us.

After his graduation from Wharton in 1961, José Miguel returned home to the Dominican Republic, and I visited him later in the summer. We were in love and though we hadn't gotten engaged or begun to make marriage plans, it was a possibility that influenced José Miguel. He felt that we should have a chaperone with us at all times to avoid the appearance of ever being alone together, in public or in private. It was important that my reputation not be tarnished in any way. My roommate, Mickey, went to the Dominican Republic as my chaperone.

I was never approached by anyone after we first arrived. Mickey and I had checked in at the Embajador Hotel in what was then called Ciudad Trujillo. As we got into the elevator, a man made a comment to me about the weather, and I answered him. The elevator operator said to him in Spanish, "Do not bother the señorita. She is the fiancée of José Miguel Bonetti."

No man spoke to me again unless José gave his tacit permission. Nevertheless, Mickey and I had a driver and a bodyguard with us wherever we went. The situation was still quite volatile. Trujillo's son, Ramfis, was serving as president and it was clear that more unrest was coming.

Mr. and Mrs. Bonetti gave a reception and dinner party to introduce me to Dominican society. Ramfis Trujillo and his family were expected at the party. When they didn't arrive, José called me out of the receiving line and said there might be more trouble. "If so, you will have to go immediately," he said. "I will send your clothes later. In the meantime, act as if nothing is happening."

Although trouble did not come that night, it was clear that there was a lot of unrest and that the country could erupt at any time. Nonetheless, over the next several days, we went on with our parties, horse races, baseball games and trips to the countryside. José Miguel's family company financed peanut growing farmers across the country, and in Santo Domingo they had a factory that processed and made peanut oil and animal feed.

As we were touring one of the plantations, I said to him, "I could start a school for the children of the workers."

He gave me a profoundly startled look.

"That will not be possible," he said. "The political situation is very unstable, and our future unpredictable. I'm sorry, but I sincerely believe this is not the moment."

We both knew in that moment, without further words, that we would never marry.

Although we cared deeply for each other, and it was hard to accept that we would not spend our lives together, it was clear that I was hopelessly unsuited for the life of a wealthy woman of leisure.

In the next several days, the unrest in the country continued to grow, and José Miguel felt it was too dangerous for me to stay. He wanted me to leave immediately, but all the flights were filled. Over my objections, José Miguel finally obtained two seats on the flight to the U.S. for Mickey and me.

Afterward, he visited me several times when he came to the United States and though we were always glad to see each other, we had started dating other people.

As I began my third year at Bartram in the fall of 1961, racial tensions in the high school and the neighborhood continued to grow. I instinctively tried to play the translator or interlocutor, explaining to the principal and the teachers why some of their perceptions, actions, and reactions were harmful to the kids. With every crisis, the principal tried a little harder to understand what I was saying.

In 1962, the *Philadelphia Tribune*, the African-American newspaper in Philadelphia, began a series of articles on racism in the public schools. At the same time, the Bartram theater department was staging its annual drama. The wildly inappropriate choice for that year was Molière's *Le Bourgeois gentilhomme*, fortunately in translation. When the play was chosen, I went to the principal to say that I felt that a play with so few roles in a school with so many kids seemed a little wrongheaded. The principal sighed, as he always did when I raised a concern, and said the decision had been made.

To complicate matters further, there were only two Black students in the play: one in the role of a maid, the other, a butler. A reporter from the *Philadelphia Tribune* heard about this and planned to attend opening night. The principal's solution was to take the Black students out of the play and simply eliminate their roles. The audience sat through a completely incomprehensible show, and the *Philadelphia Tribune* had an even better story.

After this incident, the principal agreed to my suggestion that we stage a talent show that would include as many students of both races as possible. The kids were thrilled. Music and dance were incredibly important to teenagers in 1960s Philadelphia, especially in the African-American community.

The administration saw their energy and leveraged it as a means of control. Participation in the show was contingent on following all the rules: Students had to be on time for school, keep up their grades, avoid getting into trouble of any kind, and generally be model citizens. Eager to perform, the kids complied fully.

The kids did more than comply; they designed and choreographed the whole show. I got a group of music enthusiasts together to audition the talent. Some Bartram students, all of them white, were regular dancers on *Dick Clark's American Bandstand*, whose studios were nearby. I asked some of these students to help, along with some African-American students who sang in groups or played in local bands.

We started with auditions, and quite a few students tried out. With no musical ability of my own, I relied on the opinions of the students, but I had a hard time not being able to reassure each person or group that they would be chosen.

After each audition, I would whisper to the student judges, "Can't we just accept this person now?"

The kids, always much more sensible than I was, would patiently answer, "No, we need to hear everyone. We only have so many slots."

In the midst of all this, a shy young Black girl named Patricia Holt walked onto the stage and belted out "You'll Never Walk Alone." The kids and I listened in stunned silence.

When she was done, I leaned into the kids in the row beside me and whispered, "Can we tell her that she's in the show?"

"Yes, Miss Moran, she can definitely be in the show."

Under the stage name Patti LaBelle, the young woman became a major recording star. We have stayed in touch and whenever I go to one of Patti's concerts, she either makes me stand or brings me up on stage to introduce me as Miss Moran, the teacher who had faith in her back at Bartram High. That talent show was the first time that Patti sang in public other than in church, and she says to this day that it was a breakthrough moment for her.

I sat in that darkened auditorium in 1962 and knew that I was listening to someone who would be a star. When I see her perform now, I always have a moment when I see that shy girl singing on an empty stage.

The talent show was another lesson to me in the importance of making a safe space for creativity and self-expression. Students took away a new sense of self-confidence, self-esteem, and the feeling that their peers and the world at large valued what they had to offer and what they loved. I was surprised and delighted to see how much the experience motivated the kids to succeed in the classroom, and how it brought people together in new friendships and lasting bonds.

With Patti LaBelle after a concert in New York, 1986.

Chapter 6

During 1961 and 1962, I continued to date interesting men, but I kept coming to the same realization—that I did not want to fit into any man's life, no matter how comfortable or pleasant that life might be.

During this period, I got to try out a variety of lifestyles and imagine how each might play out. I decided that I didn't want any of them. The truth was that I felt most alive and authentic with my students, and so I stayed connected to several after they had graduated.

One of these former students, an Italian-American man named Jim Brown, was a musician who played guitar and sang back-up for some of the groups of the time, including Danny and the Juniors. He was good-looking and charming and wrote some of his own music as well as some poetry and short stories.

In 1962, while he attended the University of Pennsylvania, we spent a lot of time together. My friends and I would go to hear him perform, and we enjoyed one another's company. He joined the ever-changing cast of characters at the Hamilton Court.

In the summer of 1962, I spent ten weeks in Europe traveling with one of my roommates. We spent a month in Madrid, intending to perfect our Spanish at a university. We lived in the Plaza Hotel, seven dollars a night including breakfast and dinner, and spent most of our time at the rooftop restaurant and pool. Some of the cast of *55 Days at Peking* stayed there while the movie was being made, as did the cast and crew of a German movie, in which my roommate Nancy and I got to be extras.

While there, we went to Pamplona for the San Fermín Festival and the running of the bulls, a glorious three-day party that moved from the town plaza to the bull ring to restaurants and dance halls each day. I surprised myself by being completely fascinated by the bullfights. I met a man there who had been born in Austria and brought to the United States during the War. He came to San Sebastian with me and then back to Madrid. We enjoyed ourselves in Spain but didn't like each other at all when we got back home. He took me to Homecoming Weekend at Princeton, and I saw another life unfurling before me that I definitely didn't want.

As the school year started and the world of the Hamilton Court kicked into high gear, I suddenly had a sense of "having stayed too long at the fair." I was now in my mid-twenties, and my friends were all getting married; it seemed that I was a bridesmaid every weekend for a year.

In August of 1963, I married Jim Brown, though it is hard to explain exactly why. I was twenty-six and he was twenty-one. He loved me; I cared for him. I felt that I would make his life whole and that he would do the same for me. Most importantly, I wouldn't have to change my life. He didn't want me to be a different person from the one I was.

I think my parents felt that they wouldn't lose me to him the way they might have if I had married one of the others. My mother particularly loved him. He was a very lovable guy. It was an absolutely crazy thing to do, but I did it.

I called a friend I taught with at Bartram to tell her.

"Are you sitting down?" I asked, "I'm marrying Jim Brown."

"For this I should be lying down," she said.

That was pretty much everyone's reaction, but our friends and families all came to the wedding. I wore a white Chanel suit, and Jim and his group sang at the reception at our country club.

For the next two and a half years or so, we were happy. We lived

Dancing with my father at my wedding to Jim Brown, 1963.

in an apartment in the vicinity of Penn. I went on teaching; Jim went to Penn. We spent time with my friends, and Jim was kind of taken up by a group of professors from the English Department at Penn. I once read a comment that someone made about James Dean, that he was a source of fascination and attraction for both men and women. Jim was a James Dean type: handsome, sexy, and slightly mysterious, with a strange mix of bravado and vulnerability. Although the men in this group of professors were gay, and maybe the women too, they liked Jim and me, and we became part of their social life. Although I have no idea what we represented to them, our time together was all dinner parties and charades, nights at the theater and baseball games.

Things started to fall apart in the third year as Jim was finishing his degree at Penn, and real life was about to begin. He wanted to move to California. I wanted to stay in Philadelphia, but most of all, I realized that I did not want to be married.

If we had fallen in love a decade later, we probably would have lived together and then moved on when it was over. My mother was distraught. There had never been a divorce in the family, and Jim had become the son she never had. After much carrying on, she announced, "Well, you may have been a headache, but you've never been a bore."

She became reconciled to the divorce, and then she went berserk all over again when I said that I was going back to my maiden name. "What about the engraved sterling and the monogrammed linens?"

To avoid more drama, I gave in. Today I have the name of a man I haven't seen in close to forty years, the sterling was stolen long ago, and the linens wore out even longer ago than that.

I came out of the marriage knowing that I would never marry again, that I didn't want someone else's choices to govern my life.

Although I knew there was great comfort in being with someone who loved you, and that children bring great joy, perhaps not matched by other experiences, I wanted my life to be my own. If that meant I would be alone and without children, I would accept the trades-offs.

During these same years, 1963–1967, the racially-charged turmoil in Philadelphia had increased tremendously. Bartram had a new principal who was appointed, I believe, to try to stem the white flight from the neighborhood and the school. By the time I left Bartram in 1967 the demographics of the neighborhood and the school had flipped.

The new administration was even more resistant to change than the previous one had been.

People now made decisions based on racism, fear, and blind belief in a set of rules and regulations that were completely irrelevant to the complex lives of our students. And, as the inner city grew more volatile and the school's demographics became poorer and more African-American, those racist, fearful decisions made an ugly kind of sense to many of my colleagues.

At the start of the school year in 1966, I was summoned to a meeting with the new principal. "Mrs. Brown," he said, "some of the white neighbors do not like it when you walk to the trolley stop with Black students. If a Black student starts to walk with you, you could pretend you forgot something and go back to the school and wait until the student is gone."

"I'm not going to do that. I have no intention of hiding from any of the students. I'll walk to the trolley with whomever else is walking in that direction."

"I regret that that is your decision, Mrs. Brown."

I had won that first round, but the new principal could exert his power in many other ways.

The talent show had become an annual event. At 8 o'clock on the morning of the show, while the students were setting up and their families were taking their places for the 9 a.m. performance, the principal called me into his office to tell me that he was canceling the show.

"For what reason?" I asked him, stunned but trying to maintain my composure. "I heard there is going to be trouble at the show," he said.

I answered, "If trouble starts, we will stop the show, but I don't think there will be trouble. I have no idea what you are talking about."

I felt that the principal's decision was a way of punishing me for refusing to stop walking to the trolley stop with the Black students. After arguing vehemently without success, I went backstage to tell the kids who had worked so hard that there would be no show. I was so overcome by the injustice of it that I was almost incoherent with rage. The kids were philosophical in their disappointment, but they were concerned about me.

One of them said, "I have a bottle of whiskey in my locker. I'll get it. A drink will calm you down."

"I don't think that will help, but thank you." I told him.

He looked back at me and then replied, "Mrs. Brown, if you had been colored all of your life, you would understand that you can't let things like this upset you so much, because they happen all the time."

The cancelled talent show and many other incidents made it clear to me that I would not be able to effect lasting change at Bartram. At the same time, Lyndon Johnson's War on Poverty had been launched. Programs, such as the Motivation Program, were designed to bolster academic preparation and enrich the curriculum for inner-city high school students to better prepare them for college.

In 1967, a woman from the Central School Administration who knew about my work with the students at Bartram, asked me to become the coordinator of the Motivation Program which was being launched at the West Philadelphia High School—the same school which I had been barred from working at eight years prior because of the school's predominantly African-American student body.

"I have no idea how to do that." I told her when she offered me the position.

"Of course, you do," she said. "This is what you have been trying to do for years. Moreover, this is a brand new job. No one knows how to do it. You can be the one to learn."

"I would like to try," I said, "and I will definitely do my best."

I had come of age as traditional roles for women were starting to fall apart, and new roles, like my becoming coordinator of a federally funded program, were just emerging. As a result, there was opportunity but not a lot of models and expectations. I have always felt blessed by that.

Claude McKay wrote in *Home to Harlem* that he was happy to be alive at the last moment in history when it was a true adventure to be a Black man. I feel the same way about my being a woman in the late 1950s. Growing up I had hoped I would marry a lawyer so that my husband could tell me about his work. I was fascinated by the law, but it literally never crossed my mind that I could become a lawyer myself. After I ended my marriage to Jim, I felt free to go where my life took me, and now it was taking me to a new career.

Chapter 7

In the fall of 1967, I became the Motivation Coordinator at the West Philadelphia High School. I was sorry to leave Bartram, but also excited to see what I could accomplish in an environment where I wasn't being constantly fought by the school's administration.

At West Philadelphia High School, or West Philly, as it was known, I was able to work with a principal who really cared about the school's students and shared my hopes that more of them could realize their potential.

The Motivation Program was designed on what I saw at once was a flawed premise: that only ten percent of the total student body was capable of doing college work. Therefore, all the program's resources were being used for just four hundred kids out of a school of four thousand. It wasn't hard to see that there were several problems with this approach.

There were many more students capable of college work than the allotted four hundred, and given that most of the students had gone to mediocre elementary schools, there was no way of telling that the ten percent who had been picked were the right ten percent. Moreover, the kids who made it into the program were targets of envy because they were getting so much special treatment. And those who weren't in the program had reason to feel bad about themselves.

Even though I could clearly see these problems, for the first year I just did what I was told.

The fall that I arrived at West Philly, I was invited to help fundraise for a benefit concert for the Southern Christian Leadership Conference. The concert, featuring Aretha Franklin, Harry Belafonte, and many other recording artists, was planned as a major event. Two West Philly parents who had become friends of mine, Selena Frazier and Matt Adams, had known Dr. King from his time at Morehouse College. And when Dr. King came to Philadelphia for a planning session I had the great privilege of meeting him. My friend Selena and I went to the Sheraton Hotel where he had a suite of rooms filled with his staff and donors and reporters.

Selena was going through a very painful divorce at the time and she asked to speak with him privately. He took both of us into a separate room and Selena started to cry.

Dr. King said to me, "We are going for a little walk, Mrs. Brown. Try to hold my staff off as long as you can."

A very short time later, his chief of staff started rapping on the door. When I opened it, he said, "Where is Martin?" And "Who in the hell are you?"

I was so struck by Dr. King's kindness and his concern for his friend as well as the mischievous way that he sneaked away from his obligations, if only for a few moments.

I was in Dr. King's company twice more, including the night of the truly wonderful concert. Each time I was impressed by his wisdom and compassion. Every aspect of his public persona was present in his personal interactions.

The Motivation Program at West Philly had funding for tutors, college visits, and all kinds of enrichment activities. I took the 400 students to plays, operas, and museums. Our field trips were great adventures. Some of the students had never been to center city Philadelphia, and many more had never traveled outside the city at all.

One of our trips was to Stratford, Connecticut, for the Shakespeare Festival. There was no proscenium arch for them; the plays were real. During an excellent production of *Romeo and Juliet*, one student was so engaged that he shouted out, "She's not dead," as a heartbroken Romeo was about to stab himself beside Juliet's seemingly lifeless body. I hope the actors saw it as a compliment that their performances were so authentic that the student felt he could avert the tragic ending.

The Motivation Program provided an ostensibly ideal opportunity to help the students increase their academic mastery, broaden their sense of possibility, and help them realize their potential with the goal of preparing them for college and helping them get admitted. In addition to working with students, I also started to establish relationships with administrators at local colleges, including the dean of admissions at Haverford College, Bill Ambler.

When I told Bill that one of our students, Jerome Williams, had a straight-A average, great SAT scores, and wanted to major in romance languages, he told me to be certain that he applied. Jerome immediately completed his application and sent it in. Several weeks later, Bill called to say that he had gotten everything but the school records and he wanted to set up an interview with Jerome. I apologized and said I would request them again.

After several more weeks, I got another call. Still no records, and the admissions process was in its final stages. I told Bill that I would get the records and drive out to Haverford with them.

He told me that he would be in Philadelphia the next day, and he would come to my office, review them, interview Jerome, and make a recommendation to the admissions committee.

I went to Jerome's counselor and asked for the records.

"I won't give them to you," she said. "A boy like that does not belong at Haverford."

"If Dean Ambler makes that decision, we'll have to live with it, but you can't deprive Jerome of that opportunity." I told her.

But she just repeated the same thing and refused. We went together to the principal, who said, "Give Mrs. Brown the records or give me your resignation."

Jerome got accepted to Haverford, graduated with honors, and got a Rockefeller Fellowship to Yale, where he earned a doctorate. He became the chair of the Romance Language Department at one of the public universities in Pennsylvania.

As we prepared for the second year of the program in 1968, the principal and I made two key interventions. Because we knew that the teachers needed more training to be effective, I wrote a proposal to the United States Department of Education called "Developing a Student-Centered Writing Curriculum." It would fund a program through the University of Pennsylvania to re-train inner-city high school English teachers. The teachers would attend classes at Penn in the evenings and on weekends and would receive university credit.

We also acknowledged that it wasn't fair to restrict the resources of the Motivation Program to only 400 students, so we re-structured the entire high school into four "little" schools and used the funding to support all 4,000 students. Both of these initiatives were very successful and created significant momentum for change—as it later turned out, more change than the system could tolerate.

On the awful night of April 4, 1968, I was in a yoga class and someone came and announced that Dr. King had been assassinated. I went back to my apartment in a state of shock and grief. I felt that I couldn't call my friends Selena and Matt. For the first time in my life I was conscious that being white meant that I didn't have the right to call them and offer my condolences. I was deeply grateful when each of them called me.

I also got calls from several of my students. Malcolm Bonner, one of my favorite students, called and asked me not to come to school the next day.

He said, "Some white people may die tomorrow. I might kill you myself, and I don't want you to die."

I told him, "It is my responsibility to be there and I will be."

When I got to the high school, another one of my students was waiting outside my office.

He said, "Poor Mrs. Brown, you have lost your friend."

The whole day was like that with students ricocheting between grief and rage. I asked a Black psychiatrist who was a consultant to my program to come and help the students cope. He did a series of role-plays where the students played white people hearing about Dr. King's death. The kids playing those roles, said the most vile, racist things and then sobbed or raged or both. It was tremendously difficult to experience but we made it through the day.

In 1969, as the project director for the federally funded Motivation Program at West Philly, I had a dual appointment with the University of Pennsylvania and the School District of Philadelphia, where I worked with both university and school district faculty.

After a successful year, I began working with the Penn admissions staff. I thought there was agreement to accept a group of West Philadelphia High School seniors into the university. But when the time came, in the early spring of 1970, the dean of admissions reneged on the agreement.

After six weeks of turmoil, sit-ins, pickets, and a threat to disrupt the Penn Relays, the university accepted the students. But it turned out to be another Pyrrhic victory. University personnel told the West Philly graduates that they didn't belong at Penn, and, feeling this pressure, many of the group eventually dropped out. The university also notified me that they would not be renewing my appointment as a faculty member the following year.

At the same time that we were feeling pushback from Penn, repercussions related to the re-structuring at the high school were also occurring. As it had been at Bartram, the students at West Philly were divided into tracks or learning levels based on the school's perception of their ability. Teachers who had given up trying to teach were always assigned the students who had already given up trying to learn. In this unspoken collusion, neither the teachers nor the students made any effort.

But in the new system, students were no longer tracked, which forced all the teachers to make an effort. One teacher, George Fishman, had a rule that he would not speak to Black students. His classroom methodology was to hand out mimeographed sheets, and the students would fill in the answers. If a student had a question, he would write it on the chalkboard. If Fishman chose, he would reply on the board. The students from his class came to tell me about this and offered an elegant solution. Transfer him to a school with white kids.

"No school with white kids would take him," I explained. "He's just putting in his time until retirement."

"Let's boycott his class until he agrees to teach."

I knew this could not end well, but I also knew that the students were right. All of them participated in a sit-down strike. The teacher's union picketed and the superintendent sent in the police to arrest the students. Fishman returned to handing out the mimeographed sheets, and in that moment I knew that my effectiveness as a change agent at West Philly was over.

Both the West Philadelphia student strike and the University of Pennsylvania admissions debacle happened more or less simultaneously in the spring of 1970. It was devastating to see everything we had built get blown up, to know how many kids who deserved opportunity wouldn't get it, and perhaps, worst of all, to see that sustainable systemic change probably wasn't possible.

A civil rights worker who helped us during the Fishman crisis was deeply discouraged by the results and what the implications were for change. He was also concerned that my rage level had reached a dangerous point.

"Are you ready to pick up a gun and kill white people?" he asked me one day. I was stunned at the question. "I don't even step on ants," I told him.

"Then you have to get out of here," he said. "You are on a path that leads to violence. If you stay on the front lines, you won't be able to handle your rage. You have what it takes to work within the system. That's what you're going to have to do."

I realized that he was right. The circumstances of my life had prepared me to be a person who could function both inside and outside of the mainstream.

I have been able to live my life as a white, privileged woman whose appearance and behavior can conform, if I wish, to the standards of mainstream American culture at any time and in any place. I have also, when my actions have violated those standards, been treated as less than, as the "other"—the way my students have habitually been treated.

One of my students summed this up by saying, "Mrs. Brown, you can pass for white whenever you want to." He didn't mean that there were times when I did not appear to be white, but that, if necessary, I could switch into the behavior that many of my students experienced as "white behavior."

I have met many African-Americans who have told me that they perceive white people as feeling confident and entitled much of the time. My own experience is that hardly anyone feels this way even some of the time. But it is a powerful and prevalent notion, and it exacerbates the sense of "otherness" that many people outside the dominant culture feel. Conversely, I believe that it is unusual for someone who never experiences what an African-American friend of mine calls the "indignities du jour" to understand what indiscriminate discrimination feels like.

For me, I always carry inside me what it feels like to be that little scapegoated girl with the shaved head, but I also know how privileged my life is and how comfortably I can live in it, if I choose—as well as the power of having that ability to choose.

During this very difficult time in the spring of 1970, I was dating a man named David Braveman, whom I had known in college. We were both divorced, and we were dating casually. He had graduated from Harvard Law School and was a corporate lawyer. An ardent Republican, he proudly sported a Nixon bumper sticker on one of his cars. If he brought that car to pick me up for a date, I would take a cab to wherever we were going. He had great fun talking good-naturedly about what a "bleeding heart" liberal I was.

I was at the theater with Dave one night during the West Philly student strike, and I said to him, "I am so worn out and used up that there are times when I just want to disappear into the safe, comfortable world of white people."

"What an extraordinary thing to say! What could that possibly mean?" he said. "I don't think I could explain it to you." I told him. "Let's just enjoy the show."

But not long after that evening, Dave got a glimpse of what I had been talking about. I had a date with him on a weekday evening to go to a dinner party at the home of mutual friends.

During the day, I had taken a group of about fifty tenth grade students, most of whom had never been out of Philadelphia, to the Bucks County Playhouse for a matinee performance of a Shakespearean play in modern dress.

On the way home, as we passed through the charming little village of New Hope, Pennsylvania, the students pleaded with me to stop so that they could go into the stores and buy gifts for their "Grammies" and/or girlfriends.

"All right," I said, "but hurry, we need to get back to Philadelphia by 5 o'clock."

As soon as the kids got to the doors of the stores, the shopkeepers locked them. The other teacher and I had to make an arrangement with each shopkeeper that there would only be two students in any store at any one time, and the other teacher and I would have to be there too. Something that should have taken half an hour took more than two hours. As a result, I was late for my date with Dave. When I arrived at my apartment building, he had been there waiting for more than half an hour.

"I'm sorry," I said. "Come up to my apartment and make yourself a drink. I'll get ready as fast as I can." On the way up in the elevator, I explained what had happened and why I was late. He was appalled.

"I can't believe how calmly you are taking this, Eileen," he said. "This is outrageous. There are public-accommodation laws in this country. Storeowners can't pick and choose whom they are going to serve. I hope you are going to lodge a formal complaint, maybe a lawsuit."

"David," I said to him, "I work with Black kids, and something outrageous happens to them every day. This was actually a good day. The kids loved the trip and got to buy souvenirs. No one is dead, wounded, or in jail. This is a happy ending. I don't want to talk about it anymore. I want to get ready for dinner."

David continued to be very upset and he talked about it with our friends all through dinner.

He became radicalized by a relatively benign incident in which he wasn't even personally involved himself.

In the late spring of 1970, in the aftermath of the Penn debacle and the student strike, Spencer MacDonald, the director of the Master of Arts in Teaching program (MAT) at the Harvard Graduate School of Education, suggested that I should go to Harvard, and work as a MAT teaching fellow and enroll in a doctoral program.

The Motivation Program and the project with the University of Pennsylvania had attracted his attention. He had placed some teaching interns at the West Philadelphia High School as part of their urban experience. These interns worked with our teachers and students.

I knew I couldn't stay in the Philadelphia public schools and make a difference, and I had always been troubled that my only educational training was a BA from Immaculata College. Harvard was my chance to learn how to become more effective in re-structuring public education and creating a true learning community. I decided to go.

I left Philadelphia, a city that I loved and the place where I had been young. It was a city where I felt valued and admired. A man I dated once said that going out with me was like escorting the Liberty Bell. Everywhere we went, former students, and often times their parents, stopped us on the street to tell me what I had meant to them. I left Philadelphia feeling desperate, in need of a new direction, but once I was gone, I was shocked by how much I missed the city, missed my friends and my students.

Chapter 8

In August 1970, I moved into an apartment in Cambridge, and then immediately left to visit my good friend Mickey Pugh. Mickey, my former roommate and onetime chaperone in the Dominican Republic had married and now lived in a splendid beachfront mansion in Watch Hill, Rhode Island. I stayed with her for a month, spending long sunny afternoons on the beach, sailing, attending dinner parties, returning to a version of the life of my early adulthood.

On a day in September that was clearly marked on my calendar, Mickey asked, "Isn't this the day you your classes start?"

I said, "Yes."

Mickey was silent; she had the good grace not to say, "Will you be staying in one of our guest rooms for the rest of your life?"

That night, I had a dream that an iron cover was closing over me, and if I let it close, I would be trapped forever. I fought as hard as I could to keep it open. I woke up on the floor with the beds pushed aside, the table lamp on one of the beds, the night tables knocked over, and the rug pushed into the fireplace. I was shaken by the power of the dream, but the message was clear. I was going to have to have the courage to go forward. I straightened up the room, went down to breakfast, and announced, "I'm leaving for Cambridge today."

At thirty-three years old, I was starting a new life in a city where I didn't know anyone. One of the hardest things I would learn during my early weeks at Harvard was how much it mattered to my sense of identity that I had always been with people who had known me over time. It was a searing realization for me to learn that I was shy.

My apartment was on Trowbridge Street, on the far side of all the Harvard College buildings. It was autumn, and it was beautiful. I got up every morning and walked through Harvard Yard to my classes. I felt like I was walking through a movie set or a theme park, yet I also felt profoundly disconnected from the happy "college land" in which I seemed to be living.

It's not that I wasn't proud to be there. My parents, particularly my father, were delighted. I knew that having been accepted to Harvard was a kind of validation of my work in Philadelphia.

But I was much more caught up in what I had left behind than in what I was going toward, and I was grieving for all that had been lost in Philadelphia. There, I had been sustained by the hope that I could collaborate with others to create a high school that worked and a path to college for students who had the ability to go. We had been able to do that for close to three years. But when it all fell apart, I had been devastated.

For my first six weeks at Harvard, I did not say one word to anyone outside of the classroom.

At the end of that period, another teaching fellow saw me on the street and asked if I wanted to go with him to a faculty reception that the president of the university was giving and to which we both had been invited.

"I'd love to," I told him, and I went home and cried for an hour. These were the first words of friendship that had been spoken to me since I had arrived.

After that, I began to get to know several of the other Harvard teaching fellows. Joan Goldsmith, the assistant director of the Harvard Master of Arts in Teaching program, became one of my best friends. The circumstances of her background were different from mine, but we were kindred spirits in our sensibilities and value systems.

With Joan Goldsmith, 1970s.

Joan had been born into a strong Jewish community in New York. Her mother and her father were communists, and, in the parlance of the day, Joan was a "red diaper" baby. In 1950, anti-communist fervor had swept the country; Senator Joe McCarthy was at the height of his power and the Rosenbergs had been arrested. When Joan was nine, as a way to escape some of the upheaval in New York City, the family had moved to Louisville, Kentucky.

Much as I had been taken from the comfort and safety of my nursemaid, Mae, to be shuttled among relatives and boarding school, Joan had gone from a warm, loving extended family in a city full of refugees from European fascism and African-Americans from the South, to Louisville, where she lived in a sharply segregated community where whites and Blacks, Jews and non-Jews could not easily mix.

A smart, organized, hard-working young woman, Joan had won a scholarship to Antioch College, one of the most progressive institutions in the country at the time. As a student researcher and representative, she had assisted in the revamping of Antioch, the founding of Nova University, the creation of the Great Lakes College Association, and other revolutions in higher education in the 1960s.

After graduation, Joan enrolled in a doctoral program at the University of Chicago and was active in the Civil Rights and the anti-Vietnam War movements. She organized a pre-school program with parents in a Chicago South Side housing project and soon after left to begin teaching in Boston.

In Boston, in addition to being a very successful high school history teacher, Joan also worked with a group of local educators to develop the "Vietnam Curriculum" which was published nationally in 1968 by the *New York Review of Books*.

In 1969, Spencer MacDonald, the director of the Harvard MAT program, appointed her the assistant director of the program to help him incorporate a focus on urban education into the curriculum.

Once Joan and I got to know each other, she asked me why I hadn't suggested lunch or a movie or a cup of coffee with her during my first lonely six weeks in Cambridge. She found it hard to believe that I had been too withdrawn to speak to her, even though I had realized from her comments in class and in meetings that I would enjoy her company.

During dinner at her house one evening, she commented that my energy, indeed my life, seemed to be fueled by anger. She wondered what would provide the fuel for my life if I let go of that anger.

It was a good question. I believe I held on to vestiges of that anger for many years, and it was part of what propelled me. It was anger at injustice, but it definitely had a personal element to it. Much of the sadness, despair, and vulnerability that I had felt as a child came up all over again when I moved to Cambridge. The politics and elitism of Harvard triggered the rage that I had felt all my life against the powerful forces that oppose the vulnerable.

Over time I became part of a group of friends at the Ed School that was sort of a community in exile for radicals—for creative, frustrated teachers and administrators like me who had worked in urban public schools and who had developed innovative teaching methods in desperate efforts to reach students routinely dismissed as "hard to reach," "unteachable," and "difficult."

For years, each of us had been making things up as we went along, and once we began to compare our experiences, we realized that we had all been moving in the same general direction, toward what would come to be known formally as "student-centered teaching."

In my first semester in the fall of 1970, I took academic courses and supervised graduate students who were doing teaching internships. In class, I occasionally made constructive comments, but most of the time I argued vociferously.

I found the courses interesting but not particularly relevant. The students I was supervising, including a teacher of social studies in a Watertown junior high school, were intelligent, but in many cases not well suited for teaching in public schools. The social studies teacher, in the middle of one of her lessons, asked her students how many of their parents worked at the Arsenal, a large, local munitions factory. About half the class raised their hands.

"Do you realize," the teacher said, "that your parents are responsible for killing people, including babies, in Vietnam?"

I stood up at once and said to the students, "I would like to speak with Miss Ackerman outside the classroom. Why don't you get a head start on your homework assignment?"

In the hallway, I took her aside. "That was a totally inappropriate thing for you to do. These kids are proud of their parents, and no matter how you, or I, for that matter, feel about the war, it is not for us to shame innocent twelve-year-old kids."

She glared back at me and said, "Stopping this war is the most important thing any of us can do."

"It's not the most important thing you can do in this seventh-grade class," I answered. "Go back in there and teach the lesson you prepared."

Because of my outspokenness and my ready access to my anger, I think it is fair to say that my faculty advisor at the Ed School was as unhappy with me as I was with him.

I was taking a course with him called Learning Environments. In one class, he had invited two Boston high school students, both African-Americans, who were the leaders of a student strike against the racism in the public schools, to join us.

The students thought that they had been invited to the class to get advice and support on how to make the strike successful. But unbeknownst to them, the professor had actually asked them to come because he wanted to test one of his theories on them: that willingness to confront authority was tied to social class and that people from high income backgrounds were more likely to stand up to authority.

When we had all gathered, he began asking these students questions:

"Does your father live with you?"

"Is your mother on welfare?"

"How many rooms are there in your apartment? "

"How many people sleep in one bed?"

The two students were clearly bewildered and reluctant to answer, but they also wanted the help that they had come hoping to get. When I saw where the professor was going with this, I interrupted.

"This is outrageous," I said. "What do these questions have to do with the issue at hand? Can we give these kids some help or not?"

Not long after that, the professor met with me to say that I was clearly a very successful practitioner but that Harvard was for theoreticians.

"I believe that practice has to be informed by theory," I told him. "Do you believe that theory should be informed by practice?"

"No," he said.

I knew then that I was not going to spend three years at the Ed School earning a doctorate. I would complete the year-long master's program and leave. I wanted to become more effective in creating learning communities for real kids in real schools, not theoretical people and programs.

Though my faculty advisor did not value my practical knowledge, during the year that I stayed at Harvard, I was often called upon to talk about my experiences in Philadelphia and the programs I created there.

That December, on a panel entitled "Restructuring Urban High Schools and Its Implications for Teacher Training," I described the federally-funded program I had directed at the University of Pennsylvania to retrain practicing teachers in student-centered curriculum.

One of my fellow panelists was Maureen Joy, the chair of the Education Department at Newton College of the Sacred Heart, where she and the newly appointed academic dean, John Bremer, were developing a new graduate program for practicing teachers.

John Bremer was well known as an educational innovator. Born and educated in England, where the movement for open education in schools began, John combined a deep grounding in Classics and philosophy with a talent for innovation. He had played a key role in New York City in decentralizing the public school system and the design of community-based learning centers. I knew and admired John from his work in Philadelphia, where he had created the first School Without Walls, the Parkway Program, which selected students by lottery and used the city's cultural organizations as their classrooms.

My meeting with Joy and Bremer was fortuitous; we were all interested in creating a program for training teachers that would make a real difference in the schools. I was ready to leave Harvard, and Harvard was also phasing out its Master of Arts in Teaching Program, which meant that my good friend and colleague, Joan Goldsmith, would be available to join forces with us.

The four of us had a series of meetings that winter, at the end of which Bremer asked Joan and me to come to Newton College to become the co-directors of the new graduate program, which he had named the Institute of Open Education (IOE).

We accepted his invitation. The program would launch in the summer of 1971, which left us with approximately six months to finish pulling everything together. We got to work immediately.

That spring, while I was finishing my master's degree, Joan and I invited several of the other teaching fellows at Harvard to work with us in creating a curriculum and recruiting our first class of one hundred students. Bremer had come to us with an outline of what he wanted the program to be, but he left the specifics up to me and Joan and the other IOE faculty.

This original group of IOE faculty, although recruited primarily from the Harvard Ed School, were all practitioners, as Joan and I were. We were a group of racially diverse, creative people with a range of professional experiences and a willingness to work as a team. We began building the curriculum and figuring out how the program was going to work. We put ads in the papers to attract students, and by the end of spring had completed our admissions process.

Once again, as I had done in Philadelphia, I would be able to transform some of my anger at social injustice into positive and creative energy.

At the start of my teaching career, I had learned that the ways schools had functioned for centuries simply didn't work for the majority of the students in the inner cities in 1959.

Throughout the turbulent 1960s, it had been clear that the center could not hold, that the old ways were not always the best ways, and that there was little sense of how to create new, effective structures. Education went on as it always had, and only a small percentage of students were successful. Those who didn't thrive were blamed for their failure, and because these students had already been written off, no one in authority paid much attention to what teachers did, for good or ill.

For a brief period during my time in Philadelphia, it had been possible to create positive change as long as the agents of change didn't threaten the larger system. There was a similar moment of possibility when we began to create the Institute of Open Education program at Newton that would become Cambridge College a decade later.

At that point in the early 1970s, higher education was facing some of the same issues as the public schools; most colleges were not prepared to work with a diverse student body, but in 1971 there was no urgency to adapt to a rapidly changing society.

When we started the IOE, we knew that working within an existing institution to create change was glacially slow, and for the most part, futile. The program that we introduced at Newton College slipped in while no one was particularly focused on what was happening or cared much about the results, particularly for the students we were serving.

We knew that the turmoil and the chaos of the 1960s had challenged the accepted hierarchies of patriarchy, racial supremacy, class structure, and military dominance. The Civil Rights and Women's movements, the anti-Vietnam War protests, and the social mobility of post-World War II America had affected all of us, but the widespread resistance to the changes, and the lack of national leadership and will to create new models, primarily resulted in hopelessness with some small sense of possibility.

We went for the possibility.

All of us had been involved in the struggles of the 1960s. We had learned the limits of radical behavior. The revolution would not be televised because there would be no revolution. But there could be change if we were able to exploit the system without threatening it—and while no one who could stop us was paying attention.

In June of 1971, I graduated at Harvard, and just a few short weeks later, at the beginning of July, the inaugural class of the Institute of Open Education gathered in Newton for our first workshop.

Chapter 9

The Institute of Open Education was established as a separate entity at Newton College, which had a comfortable campus in an affluent suburb west of Boston.

Because we were part of Newton, we had their degree-granting authority and accreditation. But because we had our own identity as the IOE, we also had quite a bit of latitude in working outside the traditional framework and regulations of the college.

Our goal was to establish a master's program for practicing teachers; to provide academically excellent, cost effective, and time efficient higher education to those for whom that opportunity may have been limited or denied, and to help them incorporate innovative teaching and learning models that had the promise of invigorating classrooms through student-centered curriculum. We believed, because of our own experiences as teachers, that this would support the learning styles of all students and reach those considered hard to teach.

We began with two unconventional administrative decisions.

First, as long as the applicants were practicing teachers, we did not require our incoming graduate students to have BA degrees, something that was virtually unheard of at the time.

And second, we chose to have open admissions, meaning that we accepted everyone who applied until the hundred spaces were filled.

Unlike the thousands of colleges or programs that take pride in how difficult it is for students to get accepted, we wanted to give

The Institute for Open Education (IOE) was established at Newton College of the Sacred Heart, 1971.

working adults an opportunity to assess what they had learned from their lives, to build on their strengths and draw on the resources of the IOE, the faculty and their peers, to learn what they needed to move forward in their careers and their lives. We did not want an arbitrary gate at the beginning of the learning process, and having open admissions literally removed the gate to entry.

From the beginning, we lived what we believed. The admissions process was a series of group interviews for anyone who applied. We invited prospective students to come to an information/interview session to match their hopes for achievement with what we had to offer.

The first IOE class was an unusual mix of students from the general New England area. While we mostly attracted white applicants that first year—there were only three African-American students in the class—in all other ways the diversity in age, ethnicity, class, and life experience among the students was significant.

We had progressive teachers who were working to change their school systems in radical ways; Roman Catholic nuns who had been teaching in parochial elementary schools without having completed college themselves; wealthy Catholic women who had just graduated from elite colleges and were trying to figure out what to do with their lives; women and men from Italian, Irish, and Polish immigrant backgrounds who were the first to be college-educated in their families; vocational education teachers who only had had two years of college and now needed a degree to continue teaching; and assorted others, including a graduate of Oxford University who wanted to start a school.

The richness of the group, the diversity of backgrounds, experiences, and levels of education, along with a shared eagerness to learn, and to learn from one another as well as books and faculty, made for an ideal learning community.

At least, for us at the IOE, it was ideal.

For the nuns at Newton College it was a bit of a jolt.

Newton College had appointed John Bremer as academic dean and signed off on the Institute of Open Education for one main reason: their admissions were down and they needed to increase their overall enrollment.

The times were changing, and the population of upper-middle-class white Catholic girls whom the college had traditionally served suddenly had other options.

Up until that time, many Catholic high schools had refused to send student transcripts to non-Catholic colleges. For young women in particular who came from a Catholic background, it was expected that they would attend a Catholic college.

This had been true in my own life. When I had graduated from the Immaculate Heart Academy, I had wanted to apply to Bryn Mawr College. I went to my father and asked him to challenge the notion that the academy could withhold my transcripts. Even though he was never someone who accepted arbitrary rules, his response had been that he was "afraid if I went to a non- Catholic College

I would lose my faith entirely." I wasn't able to convince him that there wasn't much left to lose.

Ultimately, his decision had been that "I could go to any Catholic College in the continental United States." So I went to Immaculata College and lost whatever was left of my faith.

But by 1971, the kind of young woman who would have gone to Newton in the past *could* now go to Bryn Mawr, or Vassar, or even Harvard (as long as she didn't mind being officially enrolled in Radcliffe). So Newton found themselves in need of attracting a new stream of students, which was in large part how the IOE had come into existence.

But while the nuns at Newton wanted to recruit different students to keep up the college's revenue, they also wanted them to look and behave in the same ways as their traditional students always had, which was to say, white and Catholic. As a result, we had some awkward, uncomfortable, and occasionally even amusing moments amongst our fairly diverse cohort of students at the IOE.

On one occasion, one of the Newton College nuns came up to the only African-American man in the class and told him very sweetly that she "had worked with his kind of people in Africa." She then turned to Joan Goldsmith and remarked that she "always found Hebrew people very energetic." It was clear that we were in for equal opportunity insensitivity and none of us should take anything personally.

There were, of course, much more serious issues that had to be negotiated, and Joan was our negotiator. She had a more mild-mannered and conciliatory approach to difficult discussions and she also knew how important it was to the success of our program that I never discuss my views on the Catholic Church, its hierarchy, or its clergy with anyone at Newton College.

As the first year of the IOE proceeded, we continued developing our courses and curricula as we went along.

We had started with the initial framework: a 15-month-long program broken into four semesters that began with an intensive summer session conducted at Newton's campus, followed by IOE faculty visits to the teacher's classrooms during the active school year in the fall and the spring to observe their teaching styles, augmented by evening and weekend classes at Newton.

The entire program would conclude with a second intensive summer session at Newton.

The specifics of the courses and workshops we developed according to what the teachers already knew and what they needed to be more successful at what they were teaching.

Workshops in particular were tailored to topics that came up in the teacher's classrooms.

John Bremer's philosophy, spelled out in a statement about the IOE, was our intellectual touchstone:

> It [is] no longer possible to standardize the courses of study that a potential teacher should pursue; there [is] too much to know, there [is] too great a variety among the starting points of the teachers, and the circumstances and settings into which the teachers [go are] too diverse. There [has] to be some way in which learning [can] be individualized, or rather, there [has] to be some way in which individual learners, the potential teachers, [can] create and organize their own learning, their own curriculum.

Our first goal was to shift the way our students approached teaching and learning. Our own individual successes in public schools had come from our ability to design the curriculum so that we the teachers took responsibility for what students learned as well as for what we taught.

In a traditional school, the teacher's role is to impart knowledge, and then to give a test to see what the student learned. In a student-centered curriculum, it is important to assess what the student knows already and then build on that with lessons that track whether the student is learning as the class goes forward.

Back at Bartram High School, James had been in the tenth grade when he had finally learned to read. His teachers in the previous nine grades had taught reading in their classes but none of them knew, or if they knew, didn't care, that he had never learned to read.

Teachers generally teach the way they were taught themselves. Our goal with the opening intensive summer program at the IOE was to help the teachers learn in a student-centered way so that they could teach that way when they returned to their classrooms in the fall where we would observe them and help them apply what they had learned at the IOE in their own classrooms.

To help our students make this shift in the learning paradigm, we began that first summer program with a series of group-learning exercises.

For one of these exercises, the entire class of 100, our six full-time faculty members, and Joan and I all gathered in a large room that served as our common meeting space to participate in a "Cardboard Carpentry Workshop."

A group of local educators from an organization called The Workshop for Learning Things, brought in sheets of triple-corrugated cardboard, saws, hammers, and nails, and—together and separately—we built tables, chairs, and bulletin boards, with the ostensible goal of making furniture for the room. But more important was our goal of helping the participants discover the different ways in which people learned. Are you a quick learner? Do you need step-by-step instruction? Do you prefer to understand the entire concept before you begin a project?

For me, anything that involved mind-body coordination was a potential disaster. I needed help every inch of the way. We intended to demonstrate to our new students—all practicing teachers themselves—that because there is such a wide divergence in how people learn, adaptable teaching and learning models had greater potential to reach more students than the traditional one-size-fits-all model.

This exercise also illustrated a central tenet of our learning model at the IOE—that each of us has things to teach and things to learn, and that none of us knows what all of us know. This was driven home by the fact that I, the co-director, had the hardest time learning how to use the tools and contributing to the building process.

Class photo at the IOE, 1970s.

A young Italian man from that inaugural class became the superintendent of a suburban school system in the Boston area. He told me that when he came to the IOE, his goal had been to become a teacher. After the cardboard carpentry exercise, he realized he could learn to be anything he wanted to be.

Later in the summer, we conducted a provocative role-playing exercise with the students called "The Schools Game," which Joan Goldsmith had created and had played with teachers from the Boston public schools. Because it was such an effective tool in helping teachers empathize with marginalized or under-performing students, it had the effect of convincing these teachers to more fully embrace our innovative teaching methods.

Before the summer program had begun, we had used the game with the IOE faculty. Norm Colb, who was the director of curriculum in Brookline, Massachusetts, a wealthy suburban school system, was an adjunct faculty member in our program. In our discussions, he argued that we were overestimating the negative impact on students when they were stereotyped by their teachers.

When we played "The Schools Game," we gave Norm the role of "Returned Dropout." He was a competitive man who was accustomed to winning, and he used all of his considerable interpersonal skills to try to earn the necessary points.

When it became clear that he couldn't prevail no matter how hard he tried, Norm threw all the little cards with points on them up in the air and said, "There is no way that I can win this [bleeping] game."

I said, "Now you know how it feels, Norm, to be defined by your race or your role."

Today, the learning modalities that have been at the core of our programs since the beginning are terms of art in schools of education: "student-centered teaching," "peer teaching and learning," "theory into practice interplay," and "supporting the student's learning starting point." But in 1971, these approaches were generally unheard of or were considered radical, innovative, experimental, anything but safe and mainstream. However, as the students experienced these modalities, they began to formulate ways to adopt them in their own teaching styles.

Our biggest problem during our first semester was John Bremer.

The program had a philosophic framework and it culminated in a master of philosophy in Education. Early in the first semester, I met with Bremer to discuss the ways in which we were integrating his philosophy into the practical approach necessary to prepare teachers for real-life classrooms.

He told me, "Once something starts, I lose interest in it. I'm working on other things. This is your job now."

But the problem was that Bremer wanted it both ways. Every week or so as the summer went on, he would object violently to something that we had done and would demand a meeting with the president of Newton College, Jim Whelan.

These meetings would quickly degenerate into screaming matches.

By the end of the summer, Whalen told us, "I am never meeting with the three of you again. I am tired of having blood all over the walls of my office."

When the summer term ended, and the academic year began, our students returned to the classrooms where they taught and enrolled in IOE courses for the evenings and weekends. Those who could joined us at Newton for weekend classes, and during the week, Joan, the other IOE faculty, and I visited them in their own classrooms to see how they taught and to conduct evening classes.

But while most of our students were teaching in the Boston area, several groups of students were located out of state, which meant that we also spent much of the fall and spring semesters traveling so that we could observe their teaching styles and conduct evening classes in their areas. In-between traveling, we worked to recruit a hundred new students who would start the following summer and overlap with the returning students.

As we were travelling a lot, the conflict with Bremer subsided somewhat but it was clearly not resolved. Then, in early January 1972, Joan and I were supervising four teachers who were located in Utica, New York, when we got a call to return to the college immediately.

We thought Bremer had prevailed, and that we were going to be fired. But fortunately for us, it turned out that he had been having comparable conflicts with other faculty and administrators across the institution.

We returned to learn that Jim Whelan had gone to the chair of the Newton College board of trustees, T. Vincent Learson, and said either Bremer goes or Whelan himself would leave.

Learson said, "I usually don't appreciate being given that kind of ultimatum, but I agree. Bremer has to go," and he did.

With Bremer gone, Joan and I returned our attentions to the IOE. As we thought ahead to the next year, there was one very significant problem that had to be addressed. Our first class of one hundred students had only had three African-American students. We also only had one minority faculty member, Ray Shepard, an author of children's books who later became an executive with Scholastic, an educational-publishing corporation. As committed as we were to the substance of our program, so too did we also want it to be as available to minority students and teachers as possible.

We were given a chance to address the Newton College Board of Trustees to request a grant to recruit minority students, and we made an impression on board chairman, T. Vincent Learson, who was also chairman and CEO of IBM.

He took Joan and me aside and said, "I'll get that funded for you, girls." We did not even flinch at being addressed as "girls."

"Thank you so much, sir. We'll send you a proposal." "Don't bother me with a proposal."

Joan and I were taken aback. "What should we do?" I asked.

"Call Dr. Tom Horton, our director of development. Come and see him and he'll report to me."

We were stunned and delighted, and so full of hope at this turn of events that we planned a fundraising trip to New York City, thinking, in our naiveté, that if we had made such an impression on the CEO of IBM, we could also get support from the Ford Foundation and other New York foundations that were committed to preparing minority teachers.

Although we got appointments, we had very discouraging visits. We did our best, but it became clear immediately that who you knew was at least as important as what you were doing.

Fortunately, we knew Learson, and we had great hopes for our last appointment in New York, which was at IBM in Armonk, on the outskirts of Westchester County, nearly forty miles north of Midtown Manhattan. We hadn't planned well, we didn't have a car, and when we went to rent one, our inexperience was in a full flower. Joan had forgotten her driver's license and we didn't have a credit card.

"We'll have to take a cab," I said to Joan. We hailed a taxi and asked the fare to Armonk.

Forty-six dollars. We pooled our money and came up with forty-seven dollars and change. "But Eileen, how will we get back?"

As sensible as Joan's question was, we had no time for rationality. We knew our visits so far had not gone well. IBM was our ace in the hole, or so I hoped.

"We'll figure it out when we get there," I answered.

On the drive north to Armonk, I had flashes of past zany adventures, but this undertaking, *The Bobbsey Twins Go Fundraising*, was a whole new level of risk and adventure.

When we arrived at the famed IBM headquarters, with its modernist design and its beautiful gardens, it felt as though we were entering a luxurious Berchtesgaden, an architecturally up-to-date wartime bunker. There were security cameras strategically placed throughout the building and uniformed guards milling about.

After signing in and smiling at one of the cameras, I asked one of the security guards if she could direct us to the ladies room. "Of course," she replied, and then proceeded to join us in the bathroom, discreetly waiting until we were finished.

When we got to the conference room, we had not been seated long before Horton asked for our proposal.

"But Mr. Learson said we didn't need a proposal," I said. I could feel that Joan sitting next to me had been struck mute by the surroundings and by the oddness of it all.

"You're coming to IBM for $50,000 with no proposal?" We had no answer to that except to repeat what Learson had told us.

"I don't think you meet our guidelines," Horton said impatiently.

Just as we began to despair, a door I hadn't seen before opened and Vin Learson loomed in the doorway. "Come in and tell me how it's going, girls." We realized that we were meeting in the anteroom to a complex of rooms, where our patron had his office. Learson beckoned to us and we did what we were told, taking the two seats across from him. He asked again, "How's it going, girls?"

"Actually, not very well, Mr. Learson," I said. "Dr. Horton feels we're not eligible for a grant, so we're pretty disappointed."

Learson turned to Horton and said, "That surprises me, Tom. I think this is a program we want to support."

Horton knew the drill. "Oh, well, I, yes, definitely. And … we have a board meeting in June. Why not get a proposal in by then?"

Learson said, "How's that, girls?"

Our fortunes had begun to shift in the last few minutes, and I lost whatever inhibitions I had left.

"Well," I began, "actually, sir, that's not too good because by June we want to have recruited the class. And we can't do that if we don't get the grant until June."

It was clear that Horton was not pleased by my resistance, but he had to answer to Learson.

"The only meeting before June is the one this Monday—and the agenda has been set for months."

"I'll get it on the agenda," Learson said and turned to Joan and me. "Can you get me a proposal by Monday?" It was Friday. Late afternoon. Now I was speechless.

Joan asked, "Do you have a typewriter?" And then we looked at each other and realized that we had definitely floated free from reality. Clearly there would be a typewriter or two at the corporate headquarters of IBM.

"Where are you staying, girls?" Learson asked.

"The Plaza." This was hardly an appropriate budget item for the IOE, but I knew that if we were fundraising, we needed to project success in everything we did. Money would attract money. That was the plan, anyway.

Learson pushed a button on his desk and said, "Don't we have a building near the Plaza?"

A voice came out of the desk. "Yes, Mr. Learson, at 58th Street and Madison Avenue." "Good. Have that open tomorrow. Have a secretary there. These girls are going to come in and write a proposal and then have it helicoptered out to me for the Monday meeting." He sat back and said, "How are you girls getting back to New York?"

"To tell you the truth, we haven't figured that out yet." I told him.

Learson spoke to his desk again, asking if anyone was driving back to New York City soon. A few minutes later, a voice came out of the desk saying that "Nick" was going in to Manhattan. When we got to the car, we were stunned to realize that Nicholas Katzenbach, the attorney general in the Kennedy administration, would be chauffeuring us to the Plaza.

On Saturday, we did everything Learson said we should do. A week later, the IOE received a check from IBM for $50,000, which we used—very successfully—to recruit minority students and faculty.

We hired an African-American graduate of the Ed School, and his recruitment efforts helped establish the IOE in the minority community. Our first class had three African-American students; our second class had thirty-three.

The IBM grant was instrumental in setting us on this course, but many of our subsequent attempts at fund-raising were much less successful. A painful lesson that I would learn over and over, as I tried to raise money for the IOE, was that fundraising is an insider's game.

It is like playing tennis with a high concrete wall instead of a net. When you lob a ball over the wall, you never know if there's someone on the other side. On the other hand, if you are invited to join the game on their side of the wall, you have a good chance of holding your own even if you are not a particularly good player. Trying to compete on the outsider half of the court can be humiliating, frustrating, enraging—the whole spectrum of feelings of the powerless.

But through this process of asking and being turned down over and over, this process of feeling hopelessly shut out, I realized that fundraising had become a new way for me to experience what many of our students felt in so many situations: the closed doors, the feeling of being unheard, the conviction that there is no other way to take the rejection except personally.

The first few years of the IOE were a time of intense learning for everyone, but I really had the most to learn. In addition to new skills like fundraising, I had to learn how to be an administrator. In Philadelphia, I had accomplished a lot but worked mostly in opposition to the people in charge. Now I was one of the people in charge.

I had joked over the years that there was an underground school for administrators somewhere and everyone learned a list of stock phrases for why something couldn't be done like, "That would establish a dangerous precedent" or "You might jeopardize our degree-granting authority."

As Joan and I struggled to make the IOE viable, I said to her one day, "I think I've gone to the underground administrator's school in my head." It was difficult for me to be the person enforcing the rules, but it was my responsibility now. So I reluctantly did what was necessary.

On the other hand, I was adamant in my response if a faculty or staff member did not share our belief that the students were our reason for being and that all of our decisions were to be made in their best interests.

During our first year, there was a faculty member who said that an African-American woman in his class was not worth his time.

I told him, "Peter, that student's tuition is paying your salary. If you can't support her learning, you can't teach here. If you want our help in becoming a more supportive teacher yourself so that you can help her, fine. If not, you should leave."

This man became a very successful faculty member. But in order for him to make the shift to accepting each student's ability to learn and his responsibility to support that learning, he needed the motivation of losing his job.

There were many times when a version of this incident occurred. In 1971, blatant racism was beginning to diminish. The Civil Rights struggles of the 1960s and the subsequent legislation had made many previously accepted behaviors unthinkable; however, the more insidious version, covert racism, remained. As a result, decisions based on race were often rationalized with other explanations.

The Institute of Open Education had a partnership with an alternative school in Watertown, and the head of the school, Dan

Poor, was one of our adjunct professors. Dan had a small budget for consultants and wanted to allocate twenty-five dollars a week for local college students to come to the school and teach seminars in subjects of interest to the students that were not on the regular roster. One request was for a seminar on African-American history.

I said to Dan, "I think that seminar should be taught by an African American." "Where would we find one?" He asked me.

"I don't think that should be difficult," I told him. "And I have a suggestion. A former student of mine from Philadelphia, Reno James, is enrolled at the Harvard Graduate School of Education. He graduated from Lincoln University and studied with Phillip Foner, a labor historian and prominent authority on African-American history. I'll get you his resume."

As was true for so many of my former students from Philadelphia, Reno was well acquainted with the vagaries of racism. When I had taught him as a senior at the John Bartram High School, I had advised him to meet with his counselor, Jeannette Pontz, to discuss his applying to college. Pontz advised him to enroll in truck-driving school.

Reno came back to me and said, "If I'm going to truck-driving school, I don't need a high school diploma. I might as well drop out and enroll now. I can help my mother support the family."

"Absolutely not," I told him. "You bring your mother up here to talk to me."

When Mrs. James came, I said, "I promise you I will get your son into college with a scholarship. Don't let him drop out of school; perhaps we can find a way for him to earn some money so he can help out at home."

She replied, "He has a paper route before school and a dishwashing job after school. He is helping enough. I want him to stay in school."

Reno went to Lincoln University on a full scholarship.

I spoke with Reno about the opportunity in Watertown and I wrote a recommendation for him as did one of his Harvard professors.

In addition, Reno asked Foner at Lincoln University to write one.

Several weeks later, Dan showed me the list of consultants whom he was presenting to the School Committee. Reno's name wasn't on it.

When I asked Dan, "Why?" he replied that Lincoln University had sent him a note telling him Foner was in Africa and would send a letter of recommendation on his return. Dan then said, "I am going to wait until he gets back from Africa before I ask for Reno James's appointment."

I actually screamed at him. "For $25 a week, you have to wait for a letter from Africa when the young man is enrolled at the Harvard Graduate School of Education and you have strong recommendations from your boss, who is an authority on re-structuring high schools, and Chester Pierce, a Harvard professor who consults across the country on public schools?"

I shamed him into presenting Reno's name to the Watertown School Committee and Reno was appointed as the first African American ever employed by their school system.

Despite these challenges, in the IOE's earliest days at Newton College, Joan and I and the program were in a splendid situation. We had a lot of autonomy and very few administrative concerns. All of our expenses and needs were taken care of by Newton College, except for scholarship money, which we continually tried to raise. We had support staff, office supplies, office space, classrooms, dormitories, telephones, a library, and the campus cafeteria. Faculty salaries were paid out of tuition fees: $2,600 per year per student. Joan and I could focus our energy entirely on designing and implementing the curriculum.

This was a very unusual set of circumstances. In the safe haven of Newton College, no external criteria were imposed on us and no financial or administrative pressures interfered with our ability to create, implement, and evaluate an effective model for teaching and learning in a diverse community.

Then, in the fall of 1972, as we prepared to recruit our third class of a hundred students, President Whalen told us that the board of trustees would probably vote to close the college as of June 1973, and that the faculty and students would be transferred to Boston College.

He gave us the option of transferring to Boston College with the rest of Newton College, but told us that he felt that, given the distinctive and freestanding nature of the program, and the fact that Boston College had its own quite traditional school of education, we might be better off affiliating with a more progressive higher education institution.

In other words, we were without a home.

Chapter 10

As Newton College went through the process of permanently closing down between the fall of 1972 and June of 1973, it felt as though the Institute of Open Education was being expelled from the Garden of Eden.

We found ourselves with a current class of 100 students as well as an incoming class of 100 and no clear idea of how we were going to be able see any of them through to the end of their degrees. Our unexpected departure from Newton also introduced us to a new range of administrative challenges we had not faced before.

At Newton, despite the occasional skirmish, Joan and I had been able to focus almost entirely on designing academic programs and working with students. But as we left Newton, we had to also learn to become tacticians and white-glove warriors just to keep our program going.

At every turn, we faced daunting administrative, financial, and political hurdles. But it was out of that extended turmoil and our fanatical determination that we created a next step and a new home for the IOE. My lifetime of standing up to authority, of never taking no for an answer, turned out to be essential for what was to come.

A thick skin was also an asset in confronting the pettiness and the slights that inevitably came our way. We were women advocating for higher education for a diverse body of low-income students. Many people in authority felt free to treat us with disdain if not contempt, and we did not have the luxury of taking offense.

As part of the transition from Newton, a team of local academics visited us to assess the Institute of Open Education. Although the quality of the program had never been in question before, this evaluation was a preview of many of the hurdles ahead. In the middle of one of these meetings, one of the evaluators, a woman, leaned across the table, put her hand on mine and said, "You want to get into our club and we won't let you."

I didn't respond. After the meeting, this same woman came up to me and asked why Joan and I had the same address. I understood her implication, but I saw no need to explain that Joan and I owned a two-family house. Although she was mistaken in her assumption about our sexual orientation, I simply didn't reply. I didn't owe her an explanation, and I wasn't free to tell her how inappropriate her behavior was.

We charged ahead one day at a time, on the lookout for opportunities and open doors, or at least doors that we might be able to push open with enough hard work and the right allies.

Along the way, at every stage, we had amazing good fortune in the people who were moved to help us and in crucial decisions that often broke in our favor.

Much to our surprise, a new home came our way sooner than we had anticipated, through Joan's association with Antioch College. As a distinguished undergraduate of the Yellow Springs, Ohio, campus, and as an alumna and consultant before her time at Harvard, Joan was well known to the president, Jim Dixon, and to vice president Morris Keeton.

Under President Dixon's visionary and unconventional leadership, Antioch had recently opened a number of learning centers around the country. He believed it was time to send the "Mother Campus," the reverential term for Yellow Springs, to the nursing home, and that the WATS line—a discount long-distance telephone service—would be the campus of the future. Long before the internet, he saw the possibilities of a virtual campus.

In the meantime, he was eager to diversify the college's student body, and rather than trying to bring large numbers of Mexican-American and African-American students from distant parts of the country to rural Ohio, he instead established Antioch learning centers in Austin, Texas, Washington, D.C., Philadelphia, Pennsylvania, and other urban areas.

Our new association with Antioch began in the summer of 1973 just as Newton was closing its doors for good. Morris Keeton called and asked Joan if she and I would serve as consultants to the Antioch-Philadelphia Graduate Center. We agreed and raised the possibility of making the IOE a Boston branch campus of the Antioch Network.

At Antioch, Dixon and Keeton were working to extend the opportunity for higher education to populations of students who were not being served in traditional colleges. At the IOE, Joan and I were working to improve public schools by training a diverse group of teachers who would be effective in the inner-cities as well as in the suburbs. The goal that we all shared was preparing more students to compete on what we hoped would be the level playing field of an American meritocracy that we believed would come.

Antioch brought together three prominent educators—Bob Schwartz, Don Davies, and Blenda Wilson—who were also committed to this goal, to evaluate our academic program.

Schwartz was the secretary of education to the then-mayor of Boston, Kevin White. A Harvard-educated leader in the school reform movement, Schwartz was helping Mayor White work through the very difficult issues of integrating the Boston Public Schools through forced busing. Davies, the former associate commissioner of the U.S. Department of Education, had been responsible for awarding the grant that had funded my programs at the University of Pennsylvania to re-train Philadelphia teachers. And Wilson was the senior associate dean of the Harvard Graduate School of Education.

It is safe to say that without the help of these three individuals at important points in our evolution, the story of the IOE might have had a different conclusion.

Blenda Wilson, in particular, became a key player in our future. An African-American woman from a working-class family in Woodbridge, New Jersey, Blenda was, like Joan and me, the first person in her family to go to college. Starting as a day-care teacher in New Jersey in 1963, Blenda had mastered the way the system worked at every step in her life journey.

By the time we met in 1973, she was a consummate inside player. Paul Ylvisaker, the well-respected dean of the Harvard Ed School, was her mentor. Through her own talent as well as with his help, she was a force in the higher education community and in the agencies that regulated it. She knew, through her own experience as a student in an inner-city school, the dismal state of education for minority students, but she was wise enough never to show her anger. She carried out all the good work she did for us over the next fifteen years with an amazing mix of political savvy and finesse.

Blenda Wilson (center) with Anne Hiatt (left), a trustee, at Cambridge College Commencement in 2000.

Just as we were developing our affiliation with Antioch, we miraculously found an office in Harvard Square and classrooms at Harvard itself that allowed us to continue holding classes during our transition from Newton to Antioch. Through the good graces of Dean Ylvisaker and Blenda Wilson, Harvard rented us classroom space at a nominal fee—in classrooms that usually sat empty at night—and gave our faculty and students library privileges. We used the Harvard classroom space and library until we acquired our own building in 1993. Our administrative offices were located in a non-Harvard building two blocks away.

But despite our good fortune in the support that we received from Antioch and Harvard, we knew that many challenges lay ahead. The immediate and most significant problem was that the student tuition would no longer cover our expenses. At Newton College, we had collected $2,600 from 100 students and used the entire $260,000 to pay faculty and staff salaries, and to buy materials, books, and anything else the program required.

By contrast, Antioch required that we give the college an overhead charge of eleven cents on every dollar we collected. The $260,000 instantly shrank to $231,400, out of which we now had to pay faculty and staff salaries and benefits, modest rents on classroom space, and market rates on everything else: office space, heat, electricity, telephone, furniture, and office supplies.

Much like a Kentucky Fried Chicken franchise pays the corporate office for the use of the name, we were paying Antioch for the right to give our students an Antioch degree. Faced with this financial squeeze, Joan and I took two dramatic steps immediately: We doubled the number of students to two hundred and the faculty in our program to twelve, and we eliminated the second summer session.

In addition to these financial challenges, we also had to get permission from the Massachusetts Board of Higher Education to award an Antioch degree in Massachusetts. We believed that because we had the same faculty and the same students that we had had at Newton College, we should be given the same degree-granting authority.

The Board did not agree and ruled that we could not offer an Ohio degree in Massachusetts. We needed to incorporate in Massachusetts and assemble a local Board of Trustees. Only then could we apply for degree-granting authority. These challenges, although onerous, turned out to be essential to our independence in the long run.

In the meantime, we called Antioch's President Dixon and reported that we had to incorporate separately in Massachusetts and asked if we should incorporate as the IOE or as Antioch-Massachusetts. His answer was typical of his radical approach, the kind of thinking that eventually cost him his job: "I don't want to create a new colonial model. I believe in supporting emerging nations. You do what you think best."

Even though Joan and I had only the dimmest sense of why it would be important to have our own corporate identity, we chose to incorporate as the IOE, with our own board of trustees, and to proceed to apply for degree-granting authority from Massachusetts. The next day, Antioch's vice president, Morris Keeton, a man more concerned with college governance than his boss, called us back and said, "Absolutely not. You must incorporate as an Antioch entity."

We told him it was too late, that we had already filed the papers. We then rushed the papers to the Board of Higher Education and began the incorporation process as the IOE. We immediately asked Blenda Wilson, Don Davies, and Bob Schwartz to be trustees of the newly constituted Institute of Open Education. They agreed.

While we waited for the Massachusetts degree-granting process to be completed, our understanding was that the students who had begun at Newton College would be given degrees. We believed that because the regional accrediting agencies have reciprocal agreements (i.e., the New England Association of Schools and Colleges has a reciprocal relationship with the North Central Association, where Antioch is based), we would be able to use Antioch's accreditation.

In September 1973, as our first academic year in Harvard Square began, we had 100 students who had just completed the summer session at Newton College and were about to be supervised in their home schools, and we were recruiting 200 more students for the following summer.

Several months into the new semester, the state appointed a new vice chancellor of higher education, Bill Moore, who wrote the IOE a letter that sent me into full panic mode.

Changing the policy under which we had been operating, Moore announced that we could not offer degrees to our current students who had been accepted under Newton College's authority, unless certain conditions were met. Members of the Board of Higher Education had to visit and assess our program, make a recommendation to the full board, and allow the board to vote on our worthiness.

I knew all of this could not be accomplished by the time our current class was ready to graduate in June 1974, and I knew, moreover, that we would be betraying both our current and incoming students if we proceeded with a program that might not be able to give them a degree.

In those days, I had no grand long-term plan to create a college. My ambition was to keep our program going for as long as possible, a challenge that this letter threw into disarray. How could we have taken our students' money, their hopes, their dreams, and now say to them, "Never mind, we can't do this after all"?

I ran crying out of my office and down two blocks to the Ed School. Still sobbing, I planted myself outside Blenda Wilson's glass-enclosed office, where I could see that she was in a meeting and she could see that I was a mess. She stepped outside and took me into another office.

"Eileen, stop crying and tell me what's going on so we can fix it."

I pulled myself together and showed her the letter and explained what I had just learned.

Blenda came to the rescue, as I hoped she would. Days later, with the weight of the Harvard Ed School behind her and in full possession of her considerable political skills, we visited Bill Moore and tried to convince him that giving the IOE interim degree-granting authority was in all of our interest.

Before the meeting, Blenda established the ground rules for my behavior. She told me that I could not rant about social injustice and prejudice; in fact, I couldn't talk at all until she gave me the signal, which was that she would move her foot away from mine.

As the meeting started, Bill and Blenda had a rather lengthy exchange of Harvard and higher education gossip. During this time, Blenda firmly established that the two of them were equals and on a first-name basis. This collegiality prevented the vice chancellor from dismissing us out of hand. He then approached the issue by pleading the limitations of his own authority.

He said, "As you know, Blenda, this is a decision for the Board of Higher Education itself; I am simply the staff person."

As he voiced this cop-out, I began to writhe in my seat with exasperation and panic, Blenda put her heel on my foot, which was the signal for "don't you dare speak."

Then she smiled at him and said, "I understand that fully, Bill; however, I have noticed that the board respects your advice very much. In fact, I have never known them to turn down one of your recommendations. I can't ask you to tell me what they will decide. I'm just asking what you are going to recommend."

Realizing that he was cornered, he sighed and said, "I will recommend interim degree-granting authority for June. One thing in your favor is that no one else has these students and no one else wants them." Within seconds, it was clear he regretted that the last sentence had left his lips.

Moore was speaking in his capacity as vice chancellor of the Massachusetts Board of Higher Education, and I knew a gaffe when I heard one.

"Mr. Moore," I said, "that will be the headline in the *Boston Globe* if the IOE does not get degree-granting authority." Blenda smiled and moved her foot off mine.

Moore's assessment, that no one else wanted our students, was sadly accurate. After we left the sanctuary of Newton College, the

IOE was more vulnerable to the overt and covert racism that permeated life in Boston in the early 1970s.

When I first moved to Boston, I had been stunned by the way people on the street would stare if a mixed-race couple or group passed, by the almost total absence of diversity at sporting and cultural events, and by the dearth of minority-group members in leadership positions in the public and private sectors. I said this to a friend of mine, an African-American woman from Philadelphia, who thought I was crazy and had forgotten our many, many battles together.

In my experience, however, the racism in Boston was different in kind as well as in degree. I asked my friend if she ever remembered white adults trapping first-grade children in a classroom, banging on the doors, and telling them with profanity-laced epithets to go back where they belonged. She had to acknowledge she had never witnessed such a scene, which had actually happened in Boston during the infamous period of forced busing to ensure school integration.

My personal experiences mirrored that difference in kind. In Philadelphia, if one crossed the boundary that threatened the white ascendancy, there were always consequences, but it was unusual for a white person to gratuitously challenge someone going about her own business.

In Boston, I was often confronted just for going about my life, if my activities included Black students or friends. One Saturday afternoon, I had finished teaching for the day, and I came upon one of my students, a young African-American woman who was studying to be a teacher, as she talked with her husband, who was holding their baby.

On his way to pick up his wife, their car had broken down. He was the coach of a youth basketball team, and he needed to get to a game. One of his young players was with him. They were trying to figure out the fastest way to get to the gym on public transportation. I said I could drive them in my car, and we set forth.

As we drove through a predominately Irish and notoriously racist section of the city, a policeman stopped me and said, "You did not come to a complete stop at that blinking red light."

I said, "I did what every other driver was doing."

My student, her husband, and the young boy began to whisper pleadingly, "Don't argue with him. We'll be arrested. You'll get hurt."

I said to the cop, "If you think I violated a traffic law, give me a ticket."

He glared at me and told me to be more careful the next time. My passengers were distraught. They told me they never should have put me in that position. A white woman driving in a car with a Black man in that section of the city was very dangerous, despite the fact that his wife and infant daughter were with us.

On a different and somewhat more humorous occasion, I once took my 80-year-old mother to the Jordan Marsh store in downtown Boston. After we found the raincoat she wanted, I said, "Let's stop in the toy department. I want to buy a Black Barbie doll for the daughter of a friend." When the saleswoman said they didn't have any, I asked if they expected any in before Christmas.

"No, we didn't order any; we only carry white Barbie dolls." She informed me.

"Don't you think that's a little short-sighted in a city where 40% of the population is African American?" I replied.

My mother, who had owned and operated a successful department store for many years, chimed in with, "That isn't very good business sense. If you don't serve your customer base, you will eventually go out of business."

This was all too much for the exasperated saleswoman who, it seemed, was braced for confrontations about race in this very polarized city. She pressed an alarm for the security guard, who rushed in to find a middle-aged woman and her elderly mother, dressed in a fur coat and matching hat, the only people in the department!

When he realized that he had been summoned to subdue us, he

gave the saleswoman a look of utter incredulity and asked, "What's going on here?"

"My mother and I were inquiring about buying a Black doll," I said, "and I think that upset the saleswoman." He shook his head and walked away.

Whether overt or covert, the IOE existed in this climate of racism.

In some ways, it worked to our advantage. None of the local colleges, public or private, saw us as competing for their desired student body.

I remember the words of a consultant I spoke to in the late 1970s, who was working on the issue of the dismally low numbers of African-American teachers in the public schools. He asked me how many minority teachers I thought the entire Massachusetts public college system had graduated the previous year. Ever the optimist, I ventured a thousand.

"Way too many zeroes," he said. "You don't even need all of your fingers to count them.

There were six."

It was very important, however, not to surrender to "reverse racism"; and at the Institute of Open Education, that was not possible. I believe that our diverse community called each of us to be our best self. If anyone succumbed to prejudice of any kind, there was a lesson to be learned.

The seventies and eighties in Boston were dominated by the crises that were caused by the busing of students to integrate the public schools. During that period, I got a call from the principal of the South Boston High School, the site of the most contentious battles over integration. The principal asked if William Leary, a security guard who was very successful in counseling young people, Black as well as white, could participate in our non-B.A. admissions process.

When we had started as an affiliate graduate program at Newton College, we had accepted Roman Catholic nuns who didn't have baccalaureate degrees into our Master's Program. After we affiliated with Antioch we continued to accept a limited number of non-BA applicants each year. These students, all of whom were working in school systems, would go through a rigorous assessment, an accelerated liberal arts program, and then go on to earn a master's degree. The competition for these non-BA slots was great, and as part of the admissions process, we conducted a group interview with all those who had applied. During this activity, each person talked about her/his life and career and hopes for the future. This group process was videotaped, and the admissions committee would view it as an additional assessment tool.

The South Boston High School's principal mentioned to me his proposed applicant, an Irish man from the neighborhood, had been a political patronage appointment for Elvira "Pixie" Palladino, a member of the Boston School Committee. Palladino was someone whom a local journalist described as "a woman whose mouth was one of the reasons that Boston was a morally uninhabitable city." This connection made the prospective applicant's support for Black students even more surprising, but I told the principal that we would be happy to allow Mr. Leary to go through the process.

At the group interview, which was conducted by our director of admissions, who was an African-American woman, Bill participated fully. However, after the interview process, during the time when everyone mingled socially, I noticed him sitting off by himself in a corner of the room.

I thought to myself that he was having a hard time competing with so many African-American fellow applicants and with having a key decision for his future being made by an African-American woman. My experience had so often been that white school personnel who were comfortable interacting with Black students were very uncomfortable with Black peers and downright hostile to the notion of a Black person in authority over them.

I went over to him and said, "Why don't you join us for some soda and something to eat?"

Bill said to me, "If you don't mind, I would like to sit here for a moment. I have had a good life. I have always been able to earn a living for myself and for my family. But I never thought that I had any hope for a life beyond South Boston, that there was no way for me to contemplate going to college and becoming a professional. I realize that I might not get accepted. If I don't, I will apply again next year; but I realize that I might never get in. But no matter what, I have tonight; I just want to sit here and enjoy the moment."

I had succumbed to the stereotype of a South Boston white man, and I got what I deserved—a chance to feel prejudiced myself.

Chapter 11

From the time we opened our doors in the spring of 1971 until the spring of 1979, Joan and I sustained the Institute of Open Education and each other.

When we left Newton College, we were faced not only with the external pressures from Antioch and the state regulatory agencies, but also with the need to do a lot more with a lot less money. For better and for worse, I lived entirely in the moment, driven by the importance of keeping the Institute alive, which I believed at the time was the same as keeping myself alive.

Despite what was happening behind the scenes, the students who passed through the IOE had a transformative learning experience. In addition to their mastery of the academic subject matter, they also learned a great deal about themselves and each other from our very diverse student body as well as from the faculty and staff. I have found that many of these incidental learnings are the most powerful.

In order for us to keep our commitment to learning from our students as well as from one another, each individual at the IOE had to be accepted as equally worthwhile. Joan and I, as well as the faculty, who had largely stayed the same throughout these years, had learned this critical lesson over and over from our experiences in inner-city public schools. In order to maintain a true learning community, you had to believe that everyone could learn.

In my years in Philadelphia, I had seen my efforts and those of the students to learn and move forward be constantly sabotaged by the structures of the school itself and the prejudices and perceptions of so many of the school personnel. Back then, when I had asked an African American friend of mine for his advice on how to change the school itself, his suggestion had been, "Bulldoze the school; turn it into a parking lot and start over."

With the IOE I was skipping the first two steps but I did see the institute as a way to start over.

Much like the teenagers whom I had taught in Philadelphia, many of our adult students at the IOE had been undervalued in their earlier schooling. It was our hope and intention to help them transcend other people's definitions of them that had been based on stereotypes and prejudice, and to help them instead define themselves by their strengths.

To help our students understand our student-centered learning model, I taught a workshop called "It's Not Where You Start; It's Where You Finish."

In some form or another, I taught it every single semester from the very first class in 1971, until I was forced to stop, extremely reluctantly, in the early 1990s when the fundraising demands for the school meant I no longer had the time.

In the workshop, I would use my own life journey as a teaching and learning exercise to try to convey that my life path had not been preordained, that there was nothing special about me. I would explain that I saw myself as an ordinary person who had managed with the help of a lot of other people to accomplish something extraordinary.

I wanted our students to understand that I came from immigrant roots. I did not go to an elite college as an undergraduate. A baccalaureate degree from Immaculata College was not exactly a passport to success. In fact, when I was at the Harvard Ed School, a faculty member had once said to me, "Imagine what you would have become if you had had a good education." He meant it as a compliment and I didn't take offense; however, what I've learned

Teaching a workshop at the IOE, 1980.

from my life is that what matters most is not what you know, but what you do with what you know.

I wanted to share with the students lessons that I had learned from my own life. My own journey as the granddaughter of immigrants to a version of an insider in mainstream America gave me an unshakable faith in the ability of anyone to make a comparable journey. I also believed that people who had struggled all of their lives to transcend difficulties and achieve success might be even more capable of adapting to change than those who had been brought up to think that they had inherited a role in a fixed society and that they could live out their lives secure in that role.

In my own life, when I had broken my engagement to the man I was supposed to marry, I had rejected the role that had been designated for me by the societal custom of the times. Many of the students in my class had done the same in their own lives.

Just as my former student Reno James had not followed his guidance counselor's designation of him as a truck driver, so many of the IOE students had gone beyond the pigeonholes in which their teachers, counselors or society itself had placed them. Now it was important for them to learn to trust the strengths that had brought them to the IOE, in spite of an accumulation of negative forces, and to build on those strengths as they went forward.

New roles were emerging and new skill sets were needed to fill them. Back in Philadelphia, when I had been asked to head the Motivation Program, I had said, "I don't know how to do that." The person in charge had very wisely answered. "This is a new job; no one knows how to do it. You can be the one who learns."

And indeed I did learn and in doing so drew on the duality that I had developed as a child of never forgetting what it feels like to be an outsider even while functioning as an inside player. Each person's journey is different, and I wanted to use this exercise to help the students evaluate their own lives.

After a discussion of my own strengths and weaknesses, I would ask the students to think about their own lives, about what they had learned from their successes and their failures and to make a list of what they thought they did well and areas in which they needed to learn. They would then form groups of four to discuss their perceptions of themselves.

Much like the Cardboard Carpentry Workshop, many students found the exercise a seminal experience, which helped them to shift the way they saw their lives and their potential. For many, the workshop was also a very affirming experience. Invariably, they would learn that they were not giving themselves enough credit.

They learned too that others often shared their same fears and hopes. One of the underlying principles of the workshop was that the ways in which we are the same are so much more powerful than the ways in which we are different.

One student, a Latino who was the executive director of Alianza Hispana, came up to me after one of these workshops and said, "If you had told me that the pain I feel as a Spanish speaking man in an Anglo world was the same as the pain of a wealthy white woman who grew up in a family where only the men mattered, I would have laughed at you. But that is what I learned in my small group tonight, and it has changed the way I look at everything."

I wanted the students to understand that so much depends on how one values oneself. I often think of a statement about this that is sometimes attributed to Maya Angelou: "When I stopped being a victim, I stopped being an accomplice." It is so important not to accept someone else's definition of who you are, not to collude in someone's attempt to belittle or demean you, your heritage, or your communities.

Ironically, after teaching one of these workshops in the early 1970s, I had an opportunity myself to experience the prejudice against the Irish that was held by earlier generations of the white Anglo-Saxon ascendancy.

During my early years in Cambridge, I had been dating a man from Philadelphia who was from a wealthy WASP family. We would alternate trips to see each other, but I much preferred to go to Philadelphia. At the time, I was living in Cambridge in a small apartment building that didn't have any laundry facilities. My friend was living in a townhouse in Philadelphia with his very own washer and dryer. As a result I would routinely arrive at his house with a large duffle bag filled with dirty clothes.

Before one of these trips, Riv—who went by a shortened version of his middle name Rivington—told me that his grandmother wanted to meet me on the Saturday night of our upcoming weekend visit. He told me to bring a long dress because his grandmother always required that her dinner guests wear evening clothes.

On Friday afternoon, I arrived with a gown in a garment bag and my duffle bag filled with dirty clothes. When Riv picked me up at the airport, he said his grandmother had gotten the days mixed up and we were driving straight from the airport to her home in Bernardsville, New Jersey.

I said, "Absolutely not. I'm exhausted. I'm in a really bad mood and I have a duffle bag filled with dirty clothes.

In an attempt to mollify me, he said, "You are not a moody person".

I said, "My ancestors come from an island where it rains every damn day. Of course, I'm a moody person".

Despite my objections, we headed straight to Bernardsville.

When we arrived, the butler took our bags while we had tea with Grandmother. After a very elaborate tea service, I went up to my room to dress for dinner and I was mortified to find that the maid had unpacked my bags. My dirty clothes were meticulously folded and put in drawers or hung on hangers. My introduction to Grandmother was not going well. Nevertheless, I took a shower, put on my long dress and went down to dinner.

After a rather odd dinner of Chicken à la King served by the butler in full livery, we withdrew to the drawing room to continue our very strained conversation. Soon after we settled in, Grandmother announced that her Irish maid had tried to garrote her, but the butler had saved her. Then she gave us a helpful tip in case any Irish person tried to strangle either of us: "You hold their gaze, keep eye contact just as you would with an animal until help arrives."

After several minutes of stunned silence, Riv attempted to reply.

"Eileen believes that the behavior of the Irish can be accounted for by the bad weather in Ireland."

As bizarre a remark as that was, Grandmother topped it with, "Really, my dear, but they're like that in good weather too."

This story was a great favorite of my father. Of course, by the time this happened in the 1970s, slurs against the entire Irish race were more of an indictment of the person making the slur than a wound to the person who was being insulted.

It still baffles me, however, that people whose ancestors had suffered so much discrimination when they came to America as immigrants could then be prejudiced against other groups. The American poet and essayist Archibald MacLeish wrote, "Races didn't bother the Americans. They were something a lot better than any race. They were a People. They were the first self-constituted, self-declared, self-created people in the history of the world." In his "America Was Promises", he wrote, "It was Man who had been promised."

    I have lived my life believing that the promise of America could be fulfilled and I wanted to play my part in fulfilling that promise. That was my hope in founding Cambridge College; to help our students to see that it's not where you start, it's where you finish.

Chapter 12

The Institute of Open Education was changing students' lives, but for me, running the IOE was an ongoing struggle. Crises large and small drove me to frenzies of action and reaction, conflict and sometimes resolution.

We had hoped that once the IOE's identity was firmly established, once we were an accredited, degree-granting Massachusetts institution, we could turn our attention back more fully to being educators. Instead everything got worse.

During our Antioch years, Joan and I were always juggling the continued growth of the academic program, the increased financial burdens, pressures from regulatory agencies, and the tumultuous politics of Antioch and its national network of branch campuses in urban areas.

The Yellow Springs' campus was a toxic mix of left-leaning rhetoric, insufficient resources, and petty personal in-fighting. There were constant struggles over finances, governance, and personalities. The central battle was between the perceived best interests of the Yellow Springs campus and those of the network.

At the same time, the network itself was its own complicated mix of agendas and personalities. In order to protect the IOE, Joan and I spent a large percentage of our time in airports and hotel rooms fighting for the Institute's survival and autonomy.

There were campuses of the Antioch Network in cities that were reasonably easy to reach by airplane like Minneapolis and San

Francisco, and in cities that were less accessible like Wheeling, West Virginia, Keene, New Hampshire, and of course, Yellow Springs, Ohio, itself. As a result, the center directors would fly to an airport that was easy to reach like La Guardia or Dulles and meet all day in a conference room at the airport.

As difficult as that was, it was always preferable to meeting in the hotels that Antioch chose.

For instance, there was a Holiday Inn somewhere near Columbia and Baltimore, Maryland, and Washington, D.C.—three cities in which Antioch had campuses. One night after a particularly harrowing day, Joan and I were awakened by the toilet in our bathroom overflowing. We called housekeeping and went back to sleep. When we woke up in the morning, we found that they had solved the problem by removing the toilet.

Joan and I got ready for the day in the rest room in the lobby. This was a particularly annoying beginning to yet another day of debilitating meetings but not necessarily an isolated example of the extreme circumstances in which we conducted Antioch business. It is amazing to realize that in the midst of all of this the Institute of Open Education continued to thrive.

The Antioch board of trustees was dominated by Yellow Springs alumni who were in constant communication with the faculty and students at the Yellow Springs campus. All of their ambivalence focused on Dixon and the network, and early in 1975 it reached a crisis point.

Although Jim Dixon was a brilliant and courageous man who had transformed Antioch from a small under-endowed liberal arts college with a declining enrollment into a national network of learning centers, the trustees felt that he had gone too far with the Network.

An Antioch graduate himself, Dixon was proud of the college's history of innovation and inclusion. Deeply committed to the Civil Rights movement, he understood that access to higher education should be rooted in the communities that it served. This was why he had set out to establish the network campuses in urban areas. His plan for Antioch's future was to create a national network which would have a two-fold purpose: increased access for minority students nationally and create additional revenue for the Yellow Springs campus.

The Antioch board of trustees wanted diversity, but not too much. They knew that the revenue generated by the network campuses was subsidizing the Yellow Springs' campus, but they didn't want the changes those campuses were bringing.

Their solution was to fire Dixon.

The network center directors pleaded with the trustees to take into consideration what Dixon's firing would mean for the survival of the network. In response, the trustees would proclaim, "We are completely committed to the network."

At one of these meetings, I asked, "How can the network continue to thrive without the wisdom, the vision and energy of the man who created it?"

The trustees believed that they could find a more traditional president who would be able to achieve the same results but without all the change. As a result, Dixon was fired, and any hope that there would be a long-term plan for Antioch's future left with him. The vice president at the time, Morris Keeton, was the obvious person to become president, but the same factions that fired Dixon blocked that appointment.

The presidential search committee was composed of a large group of Antioch trustees and university personnel, and I was a member as a representative from the Network. The meetings were very contentious and the opposing views of what Antioch was and what it could become were clear in every interaction.

One small incident served as a microcosm of the committee's differences. After having sifted through an amazing array of resumés, including a woman who had been a perennial beauty pageant contestant who was ready for a new career and a man who was willing to postpone opening his bicycle shop if appointed, we were interviewing finalists.

During the interview process, one of the finalists, a community college president who wanted to "step up" to heading a private college, was asked, "How would you handle the time management issues in a much larger institution?"

His answer was, "I have a very good girl who takes care of me and I will bring her along."

Congresswoman Eleanor Holmes Norton, who was an Antioch graduate and was on the committee, said, "We do not need to hear anymore from you; thank you for coming in."

Several men on the committee were outraged.

"You were rude to that man, perhaps the woman doesn't mind being called a girl. This is political correctness."

Eleanor Holmes Norton, Congresswoman, District of Columbia. She received an honorary degree from Cambridge College.

Eleanor's answer was, "No, this is common sense. No matter how he refers to her or how she feels about it. If he can look around this table, filled with powerful women and not have the sense not to refer to a grown woman as a girl, he would not last a day at Antioch."

After interviewing all the finalists, a group of us, including Congresswoman Norton, said, "None of these candidates can provide the leadership Antioch needs to go into the future. We have to extend the search. Morris Keeton can continue to serve as the interim president until we find the right person."

The chair of the committee replied, "One of these men is going to be the next president of Antioch. Pick one."

Congresswoman Norton left in protest, and we picked William Birenbaum. I have always felt that the beginning of the end of Antioch started on that day. Although several of the network campuses still survive, the main campus closed about thirty years later.

In 1979, along with of all the turmoil with Antioch, the Institute of Open Education faced yet another challenge: Joan Goldsmith had decided to move to the West Coast.

Joan and I had had a powerful, productive, symbiotic partnership that had helped us survive eight very difficult years of keeping the IEO running. I respected and supported her decision to leave, but the prospect of carrying on alone was terrifying.

Joan and I had very different skill sets. I have always felt that my own range is narrow but deep. In those years, I thought of myself as a person with a few significant talents—though it was hard to pinpoint what they were—who was also often crippled by anxiety and anger.

My public face, when I was teaching or running the IOE, was that of a serious, deeply engaged professional. But in my private time and in the recesses of my psyche, I was coming to understand more about my deepest vulnerabilities. When I read about Aretha Franklin, I instantly identified with the idea that there were two parts of her being: her magnificent public voice and a private self that her audience would never have imagined. At times she was so full of fear, she had trouble leaving her house.

As I faced the prospect of running the IOE without Joan and her many strengths, I found myself in the awkward mode of trying to figure out more precisely what my own talents were. I knew that I connected with people in a profound way. If I believed in something, I could sell it to almost anyone, even if it was only a dream. Over the years, I had acquired and sharpened my political skills. In most situations, I was able to figure out what mattered most in time to make pretty good decisions. I was, and still am, a fighter and a survivor.

But as Joan and I looked realistically at the prospect of my leading the IOE without her, we both felt hopeless. I contemplated what lay ahead: the continuing battles with Antioch, the constant financial pressures, and the internal struggles with our faculty. It had been so hard for the two of us to sustain the IOE. It was unimaginable to think that I would be able to provide the leadership for it by myself.

After many hours of anguished discussion in our offices in Harvard Square, we reached the decision that we would leave together and that Antioch could appoint a new director. The next step would be to convene our board of trustees, tell them the news, and help them figure out how to proceed.

The IOE had an attorney in those days who would preface every conversation we had with the line: "Eileen, let's try to resolve this situation with your head instead of your heart."

After I made the rational decision to resign with Joan, I left the office and walked the mile to my house. By the time I got home, I knew that I had to keep going for as long as I could—and let my heart prevail instead.

This decision was the beginning of what I always call "the difficult middle-years," a ten-year period that stretched from the late-1970s to the late-1980s, in which I struggled on an almost daily basis to figure out how to continue.

Over and over, I would come to the conclusion that the task was too daunting, and then realize that I couldn't stop doing what I had been doing since the day I first walked into John Bartram High

Through stressful times, my dogs have always kept me sane.
Here, with Prince and Tiger, in the early 1980s.

School and met the students who changed my life.

After many rounds of these painful deliberations, I came to understand that although mine was not a religious calling, I was committed to the mission of the IOE to the core of my being. Hard as I knew it would be to manage without Joan, I eventually accepted the idea that I would have to learn how to do just that.

In the early spring of 1979, I became the sole director of the IOE and assumed the title of an Antioch College dean.

Soon after, we learned that Antioch needed $3.3 million in cash by June 30 or their vendors would put them into Chapter 11. Days later, the new Antioch president, Bill Birenbaum, called a meeting in New York City of the leaders of the Yellow Springs campus and of the Network centers. He announced that he intended to "save" $1 million of the $3.3 million by not meeting the May payroll. The room was silent, but not for long.

I announced that I would not go along with this. Bill was livid, and rightly so. Although the IOE was an academic showcase for Antioch, we were also part of the problem, in that we had a deficit, as did some of the other network centers. I insisted that there had to be another way to solve the problem: either sell some real estate or get a loan from a major donor.

I also got Bill's attention by reminding my colleagues that Antioch spent $1 million a year to house him in New York City despite the fact that there were no Antioch programs in all of New York state. Because Bill did not want to move to Yellow Springs, the college paid for all his living expenses, including a car and driver in New York City.

Later in the meeting, I heard one of the financial advisors say, sotto voce, "The plug has been out of this bathtub for a long time."

Afterwards, Bill took me aside and told me not to mention his living situation again. He promised that we would try to work something out about the IOE May payroll, but I was not to say anything in public about that either. I was to pretend to go along with his money-saving strategy. Collusion was the name of the game at Antioch at the time. Side deals were constantly being struck.

Throughout the month of May, Birenbaum called and tried to convince me to make some kind of compromise; pay people I thought were hardship cases, pay faculty but not staff.

"The only paycheck I'll hold back is my own," I said.

In the meantime, I convened the IOE Board of Trustees, told them what was happening, and asked their permission to deposit our May tuition money in the IOE account that was separate from the Antioch/IOE account to which Antioch had access. The Board agreed.

Birenbaum told me that if I met the payroll, he would fire me.

"I'm going to do what I need to do," I answered, "and you'll do what you need to do."

He replied by sending Ralph Wolfe, dean of the Antioch Graduate School, to Cambridge to try to change my mind. It didn't work. I released paychecks, as usual. And I wasn't fired. But I knew I would not be able to function effectively as the dean of Antioch/IOE for much longer, and I knew that if someone from Yellow Springs was sent to replace me, the institution we had built would be ruined.

At the June 1979 meeting of the Antioch board of trustees in Washington, D.C., a trustee pledged the remaining $2.3 million that would allow Antioch to avoid bankruptcy for the moment, but it was clear to me that there was no long-term plan, nor would there be, to resolve the college's complex troubles.

I left the meeting certain that becoming a freestanding institution was our only hope for survival.

Back in Cambridge, I convened a meeting of our own board and recommended that we begin the process of becoming an independent, fully accredited institution.

I knew how difficult it would be to become accredited, but I felt that the IOE was in a strong position to strike out on its own—we were incorporated separately and we had our own degree-granting authority. Most important of all we had a committed, hard-working, and powerful board of trustees who understood how radical an enterprise we were undertaking together.

Our new college was intended to be a distinctive institution, one that would serve working adults for whom the opportunity for higher education had been limited or denied. The trustees and I had endless discussions about how to achieve our goals. The faculty and I had heated disagreements about many things but never about the mission itself or the educability of our students. I knew that our sense of shared purpose was fundamental to our survival and our success.

Very fortunately for us, one of our board members, Peggy Dulany, was a daughter of David Rockefeller. In 1977, while a doctoral student at the Harvard Ed School, Peggy's strong interest in alternative education led her to join the IOE board. She had been elected chair of our board in 1979, shortly before the latest Antioch crisis. Although Peggy had given up her family's surname, she could not help but bring with her the influence of her family and the possibility of its financial help.

Peggy Dulany, along with Joan Goldsmith and Blenda Wilson, became one of the people without whom Cambridge College would not have come into being.

Like Joan, Blenda, and me, Peggy had a distinctive and powerful ability to move seamlessly between two quite different worlds. As a member of one of America's most prominent and wealthy families, Peggy was the ultimate insider. She was also deeply compassionate and had a gift for connecting with people different from herself.

In the early 1980s, Peggy gave an address to our graduates entitled, "Finding One's Own Voice," in which she talked about her struggle to achieve her own identity in the context of the Rockefeller family. In her speech, she stressed how each of us struggles in the context of a larger identity.

With Peggy Dulany at Pocantico, 1980s.

The plan to break away from Antioch was more of a complex evolution than a single decision. Looking back, I realize there was no one moment when all the elements crystallized into a neat package. It was through a mix of hard work, devoted and powerful friends, great timing and good luck that we were able to achieve everything needed to be independent: degree-granting authority, accreditation, and eligibility for federal financial aid. But I have always believed that the most important factor was the rightness of what we were doing; the need for an institution like ours.

During the eighteen months that it took the Institute of Open Education to become a college, we tried to decide on a name.

Open Education College?

Open College?

Open Education Institute?

New College?

I hated every one of those names, but we had to make a decision.

A small group of trustees and I sat down and vowed not to leave the room until we had decided on our new name. Everyone started kicking around more variations on the IOE name and then someone said, "Cambridge College."

As a group we knew immediately that it was the right name; Cambridge College established our connection to our community. It seemed as if we had all already known our name in our hearts and just hadn't said it out loud yet. In fact, no one remembers for sure who said it first.

Blenda Wilson pointed out that, "Cambridge College is really a community organization turning itself into a college."

I liked her formulation because I knew that many of the students we served needed a community-based organization rather than a traditional ivory tower institution.

By 1981, we had our name, our degree-granting authority, and our accreditation. We thought we were home free, but there was one more hurdle.

It was our understanding that once we had received our

accreditation, we only needed to alert the U.S. Department of Education to our new status so that our students could apply for financial aid and federally guaranteed loans, which a high percentage of them would need.

When we had begun the accreditation process in 1979, a college's eligibility for financial aid came automatically to any accredited institution. In 1981, after we received our accreditation, I made a call to the Department of Education and was told that the newly installed Reagan administration had changed the guidelines: colleges now had to have assets greater than their liabilities for their students to be eligible for loans and aid.

We'd been one step away from the finish line until this phone call. Now it was miles away.

I panicked, but by this time, I was a more seasoned player. Instead of sobbing outside Blenda Wilson's office, I picked up the phone and called three people prominent in higher education who were familiar with DOE politics. One by one, they told me a version of the same thing: You'll have to play the Rockefeller card at the White House.

As a backdrop to everything we had done since Peggy had joined our board of trustees—dealing with state and federal agencies, recruiting trustees, faculty, and students, and even renting office space and buying supplies—was the financial and political power of the Rockefeller family, as well as the implication that if something went wrong, the family would come to our rescue.

I couldn't count the number of times I was asked that question: "Will the Rockefellers come to your aid if all else fails?" My answer, said with optimism and a team spirit borne of all those football games with my father, was always, "I hope so." Now I was going to have a chance to find out.

With great reluctance, I called Rick Salomon, David Rockefeller's senior staff person, and asked if he would ask David to intercede for us. At first, he balked.

"David hates this kind of naked use of his power," he said, "and he's out of the country."

I didn't want to ask any more of the family than I already had, but I couldn't walk away when we were so close. Using all of my skills of persuasion, I managed to convince Rick to explore the situation himself. He phoned a former Rockefeller staff member who worked at the White House and called me back to report that this man had said the three little words we needed to hear: "I'll fix it." And he did.

In 1981, Cambridge College officially became an institution of higher education in its own right, and I was its first president.

Chapter 13

Throughout the process of becoming an independent college and well into the future, there was always financial tension and uncertainty. We didn't want to raise the tuition, and we didn't want to compromise the academic quality of the program.

It was clear that without Antioch's cash flow as a backstop, we would have to raise a considerable amount of money through gifts and grants. As we began to forge our new identity, the trustees told me that I would have to do even more fundraising than I was doing already.

I dreaded the prospect.

"There is a reason that I live alone with a dog," I explained to the board. "I can't bear rejection, and that's what happens when you ask for money."

But I told the trustees I would do my best. And I did.

But my best would not have been good enough without Peggy Dulany, who said, when the hour came, "Now it's time to put on our high-heeled shoes and go ask for money."

Our initial fund-raising adventures were amazing learning experiences, and most of what I learned or re-learned is that foundations exist in an elite, sealed-off world, inaccessible without insider connections. Fortunately for us, Elizabeth McCormack, the philanthropic advisor to the Rockefeller family, became our guide to that world.

As was the case with each of the key players in the founding of Cambridge College, Elizabeth McCormack was a remarkable person with a distinctive life history. As a Roman Catholic nun, she had been the headmistress of the Academy of the Sacred Heart in Greenwich, Connecticut, and, from 1966 to 1974, the president of Manhattanville College in Purchase, New York. From the 1950s to 1970s, these institutions educated young women from the elite of the Catholic world. In 1974, Elizabeth left the convent and married. Several years later, she became the philanthropic advisor to the Rockefeller family.

Elizabeth had the deep understanding of the nuances of power that only comes from experiencing the exercise of power in the arenas where it counts. As a member of the Catholic hierarchy, a Rockefeller-family insider, and a member of corporate and foundation boards, she had learned to leverage power more skillfully than anyone I'd ever known.

She had the ability to read the subtext of a situation, to figure out what was really going on as opposed to what appeared to be going on. On one occasion, she had written to the president of a foundation with which she was affiliated to request a modest discretionary grant for Cambridge College. When she asked me the status of the request, I said, "I think it's going to be good news. I called the foundation and was told by the assistant that the president is discussing it with the chairman of the board today."

"That's not good news," she replied. "The president doesn't need to ask permission to approve my request. He needs permission to deny it."

Sure enough, while we were meeting, Elizabeth got a call from the foundation president to tell her how sorry he was that Cambridge College didn't meet their guidelines.

"Isn't that the point of discretionary grants?" she replied and hung up the phone.

It was my good fortune that Elizabeth was willing to share her knowledge with me since the earliest days of our acquaintance. In fact, back when we met there was so much for me to learn that we established the ritual of a weekly phone call every Sunday at 12:30 p.m. For close to thirty years, each phone call was an exchange of interesting odds and ends, a mentoring session, and a mini-exam.

In addition to knowing amazing things about everybody and everything, Elizabeth reduced the most complicated situation to a clear piece of good advice. On one of our Sunday calls, I was feeling very sorry for myself about whatever the problem of the moment was.

"Eileen," Elizabeth said, "you are dealing with problems that the ordinary college president could never imagine, but you have none of the regular problems."

It was a very consoling thought. Since then, whenever I read about an out-of-control fraternity, a campus hate crime, or a scandal in an athletic department, I think of Elizabeth.

She also never hesitated to let me know what she thought. Whenever I talked too long at a board meeting or an event, she would begin to tap her watch. And she had a special talent for assessing people quickly. I once put a prospective development director beside her at a dinner party to get her opinion of his suitability. When I went up later for her opinion, she turned to me and said "N-O" and then moved on to another conversation.

Early on, Elizabeth told me, "Fundraising is an art, not a science." Over the years, however, she not only helped me to master the art of fundraising, but also taught me how to use the tools necessary for success. As indispensable mentor and a close friend, Elizabeth supported both Cambridge College and me for nearly three decades.

But in the late 1970s, when Elizabeth arranged our first fundraising trip to the Rockefeller Foundation, I had no idea how crucial a figure she would be in my life and in the evolution of Cambridge College. I was simply grateful that she had gotten us an appointment.

That morning, Peggy and I flew down from Boston for the day. While we sat in the foundation reception area, Peggy asked the woman behind the desk if she could place a call to check on her young son. He'd been sick when she left Boston that morning.

"There's a pay phone in the lobby," the woman said sharply. After a long wait, the program officer came out to meet us.

"I'm sorry, I have very little time to spend with you," she said and whisked us down to the cafeteria. "I'm not sure why I was asked to see you."

Slightly dismayed, Peggy and I tried to explain our innovative school, our ambitious programs for retraining practicing teachers and for increasing the number of minority teachers in the public schools. After hurrying us through the food line, she sat us down and asked how we knew Elizabeth McCormack.

"She works for my family," Peggy said matter-of-factly. The program officer was startled—but still irritated with us. "How are you related to the Rockefeller family?"

"I'm David's daughter."

I was afraid the poor woman might choke on her salad. Her transformation was instantaneous. She asked if we had time to meet a few people and proceeded to take us from office to office, introducing us to every important officer of the foundation, including John Knowles, the president. At each office, she fawned all over Peggy while hinting broadly that Peggy was "a member of the family."

My favorite moment came as we left when the receptionist rose from her chair to inquire, "May I place a call for you, Ms. Dulany?"

When we got to the elevator, Peggy said, "That was so much worse than my worst nightmare."

As I look back on my early years as a reluctant fundraiser, I remember that in those days, the amount of the gift was in inverse proportion to the amount of time spent actually talking about the college. When one of Mr. Rockefeller's senior staff members accompanied us on a visit to the Exxon Corporation, the conversation was about the Rockefeller oil fields in Venezuela and the sad state of Red Sox pitching. As we left the meeting, I was completely bewildered and I asked the Rockefeller staff member what would happen with our grant proposal.

"You'll get $50,000," he said. And we did.

Peggy and I did a version of our first New York trip for years and raised millions of dollars from many foundations and generous individuals. In many cases, we had introductions from Elizabeth McCormack—and the imprimatur of both the Rockefeller family and Harvard, where our classes were held until 1993.

The Rockefeller family did more than make financial contributions and introduce us to other sources of funding. Over the years, they have been extraordinarily generous in giving us the use of various locations to hold fund-raising events. In their splendid offices in Rockefeller Center, a grand Art Deco apartment above Radio City Music Hall, and the rolling hills, tennis courts, and beautiful buildings of the family estate in Westchester County, New York, I have promoted the college to hundreds of wealthy men and women interested in social justice and educational equity.

At one particularly memorable event in the penthouse at the top of Radio City, two of my former students from Bartram, Patti LaBelle and Earl Monroe, were among the guests. Patti, as always, was one of the stars of the evening. However, Earl was instrumental in securing a major donor for the college. David Koch, the billionaire vice president of Koch Industries, had been invited by one of the college's trustees, Tom Gerrity, who had been a classmate of David's at MIT. Unfortunately, Tom was not able to attend.

When David was about to leave, I persuaded him to stay.

Then he asked, "Is that Earl Monroe?"

I said, "Yes. Would you like to go one-on-one with him for $50,000?"

He said, "Absolutely."

I told Earl, who responded, "Eileen, my knees are shot. I don't play basketball anymore."

"Better yet," I said. "Let him win!"

They had lunch in lieu of the proposed time on the parquet. David Koch gave Cambridge College that $50,000 donation and, over the years, $2 million more.

As crucial as the Rockefeller family and others have been to our

With David Koch, c. 2002.

survival, there were many tough times over the years when I was not sure that even their help would be enough to overcome the hurdles and the rejections we faced. I say "we," because the college was a community of trustees, faculty, and students, but as the president, I was always on the front lines, always asking for money and always responsible for handling the outcome, whatever it was.

There were so many times when I felt that I could not keep trying to create possibility and hope when there was so much money that had to be raised and so many legitimate questions about our ability to survive over time. At each of those times, one of our trustees, our donors, our students would find a way to help me go on.

The pattern for this cycle had been established in early 1979 right after Joan Goldsmith had decided to leave for the West Coast: a pattern of hopefulness followed by a devastating rejection and then the encouragement and strength to go on.

Six weeks after my father died, I was in New York City for an important foundation meeting.

My mother was also in Manhattan that day, and we met for lunch. We were both mourning the loss of my father, and I lost track of time. When I realized I might be late, I hustled my grieving mother through lunch and left her to go to my appointment. When I finished my presentation at the foundation, the foundation official's reaction was one I had heard before, but with the loss of my father, and my mother grieving alone in a nearby hotel, it hit me hard.

"There's no way you can make this school happen," the woman said. "You're talking about raising millions of dollars. We only give that kind of money to established institutions. And how do you know you can survive over time? What makes you think you can prepare minority teachers when so many major, heavily funded universities fail?"

I don't remember what I said in response. I like to think I had an upbeat speech for her, and maybe I did. But what I remember about that day is what happened once I left the foundation. I had a plan to meet Peggy Dulany at her family's office at Rockefeller Center, and then I would return to my mother. While I waited for Peggy in a small conference room outside her father's office, I felt so hopeless that I sat with my head in my hands, and I felt I simply couldn't keep going this way.

My spirit wasn't strong enough to keep the whole project moving forward anymore. We had all believed so strongly in creating possibility out of no possibility, and we'd made it work for a while. I knew the college could survive for a few more years, but I could not see a way that I could turn it into a place that could thrive over time. I just wasn't strong enough to make that happen, and I had no good answers to the questions I always got about the future. I knew too that it wasn't fair to keep counting on the Rockefeller family to sustain us.

I raised my head, took a deep breath, and was startled to see that I was looking across the table at a Marc Chagall painting hanging on the wall. Sitting alone in a small room with an original Chagall is a very calming experience, and in that calmness I felt some of my angst and self-pity fall away.

It was true that if I gave up, the college would lose its forward momentum and I realized I couldn't let that happen. There were other people who cared about the students and our mission, but no one who was in the position that I was in, and no one who could move as easily as I could between the two worlds, between the haves and the have-nots.

In those few moments, I understood that everything in my life up until then—my family history, my scarred childhood, my intense connection to my students from the day I began teaching, my society parties, even my exotic love life—all of it had prepared me for being the person I had become, and the person who was destined to

In New York City: (left to right) Earl Moore, Cambridge College alumnus, me, Patti LaBelle, Oscar Oramas, Cuban Ambassador to the U.N., and Peggy Dulany, 1980s.

make Cambridge College work. The problem was a practical one: I really didn't know how to make it succeed. But I didn't know how to stop trying either.

At that moment Peggy came into the room looking much more elegant than usual, wearing a beautiful suit instead of her Cambridge casual attire.

I said, "You look like a million dollars." She said, "At least."

Peggy didn't usually take such a light-hearted approach to her wealth, and we both laughed.

Then she noticed my look of exhaustion and semi-defeat. "What's wrong?" she asked.

When I told her, she sat beside me and said, "We'll figure out how to go forward. We are not going to let these students down."

There was still much more to do to make Cambridge College the thriving institution it is today, but in that moment, having faced the darkest possibility that I would give up, I also knew that I cared too much to let that happen.

Chapter 14

For much of the 1980s, the structure of Cambridge College closely resembled what it had been as the Institute of Open Education. We offered one degree, a Masters of Education, and until 1988, our enrollment hovered around three hundred students a year.

Although our original intention as an institution had only been to provide a master's level program for practicing teachers who could not afford to leave their jobs to go to graduate school, we learned almost immediately that there were adults who were working in human and social service agencies, and counseling centers as well as public and private companies who were also eager to become more effective professionals by increasing their knowledge base and skill sets.

As a result, during the eighties and early nineties—we extended our programs to these professions. While still only offering a Masters of Education, we expanded the college so that it had three departments instead of just one.

In addition to the obvious mission of the education department, our counseling psychology program was for those working in social service agencies, school guidance counseling departments, and therapy practices, including addiction counseling. Our graduate program in management was for students who wanted to become managers in both private and public sector organizations.

In expanding our curriculum beyond the area of education, we adapted the key elements of the teaching and learning model we had created at the IOE and refined at Antioch. We designed a curriculum that combined the academic subject matter relevant to the particular field, peer teaching, and the theory-practice interplay elements of our model. We accepted as students only those professionals who were already working at some level in the fields of counseling or management.

Many of the original IOE faculty and IOE board of trustees had carried over to Cambridge College, and we still vividly remembered the years we had spent working in public schools ourselves, where we had learned the importance of having at least a few community-based teachers who understood some of the same issues of race and poverty that their students faced, and had overcome these barriers to become teachers themselves.

Over the years, many of the students who have gone through the counseling and psychology program at Cambridge College have done just this; transcended difficult life situations and come to the College to gain mastery of cognitive content to help others face the same issues they themselves have experienced.

Recovering alcoholics and addicts have started careers as treatment specialists and substance abuse counselors. Women who became pregnant as teenagers have gone on to work in teen pregnancy prevention programs. We have also had several students who have experienced homelessness learn the skills to be able to start their own shelters.

One former student, Kattie Portis, a former drug addict, went on to establish Women, Inc., the first residential treatment center for drug-addicted mothers and their children and later became the policy advisor on substance abuse prevention to Mayor Thomas Menino of Boston, where she was a very credible and powerful spokesperson.

I remember a panel she served on in the eighties with some experts in the field of "at-risk" children. One of the panelists was advocating re-instituting orphanages. Kattie spoke not only from her

Ben Thompson, me, Kattie Portis and David Rockefeller, Jr., 1980s.

own experience of being able to recover from drug addiction only because of her love for her child, but also from all she had learned helping other women recover while their children stayed with them. Her eloquence on the power of the bond between mother and child silenced the experts.

Another student, Ben Thompson, was a former convict who graduated from Cambridge College and became the first penal commissioner in the history of the country to have been in prison himself. The McNeil/Lehrer Report did a segment on Ben when he was in charge of the Deer Island House of Correction in Boston Harbor.

One of the inmates who was interviewed said, "Nothing that anyone has ever said to me about changing my life has convinced me that that was possible until I discovered that Ben Thompson was in a cell like me before he became the man in charge."

Thompson went on to become the executive director of Strive, a

John Bell received an honorary degree from Cambridge College.

job training and placement program in Boston for former convicts, many of whom he sent to Cambridge College.

In our management program, we have had many students who had been identified by their supervisors at work as having leadership potential. After completing their studies, they have often assumed new roles in their companies. One such student, John Bell, attended Cambridge College while working as a lineman for the New England Telephone Company. He then went on to become executive vice president for human resources at Verizon.

It was the diversity of the student body, the unusual mix of faculty members, and the distinctiveness of the learning model that made it so difficult for me to find a partner who even approached Joan's caliber and experience.

During the eighties and early nineties I appointed three successive vice presidents who each came from traditional institutions. Each one had a difficult time for his own reasons and left after several years.

The daily pressure to make it all work, particularly with a faculty that was opposed to authority of any kind, was too much to ask of administrators from more conventional schools.

My own leadership style was strong enough to hold the college together, but not enough to build long-term structures. Warren Bennis, the former president of the University of Cincinnati and chairman of The Leadership Institute at the University of Southern California, had been one of our trustees since the early days. Shortly after he finished writing a book on leadership, for which he had interviewed scores of corporate and non-profit leaders, he gave a speech at Cambridge College where he said, "I've found most institutions to be over-managed and under-led. Cambridge College is the only one I've found that's over-led and under-managed."

Even though it seemed impossible to for me to find a partner who could match Joan, the outstanding quality of our board of trustees—a group of distinguished and engaged people concerned with education and social justice who committed time, wisdom, and money to Cambridge College above and far beyond the call of duty—was one of the important constants throughout this tumultuous period.

In addition to Peggy Dulany, our board grew to include Jonathan Z. Larsen, a prominent journalist and former editor of *New Times* magazine and editor-in-chief of *The Village Voice*, and Anne Peretz, an artist and the founder of a social service agency in Somerville, Massachusetts, called The Family Center, which today is a national organization known as Parenting Journey.

Both of them joined Peggy, Elizabeth McCormack, and me in taking the college into the future.

Cambridge College conducted classes for many years in the Harvard Ed School's Larsen Hall, dedicated to Jon's father, Roy Larsen, the former president of Time, Inc. Throughout the years, both Anne and Jon have been people who have been there for the good times and especially for the bad.

In most colleges, the president reports to a board of trustees on the successes and challenges of an institution that has been operating

Jonathan Z. Larsen, c. 1990.

for decades. At Cambridge College, these four trustees were with me every step of the way as we built the college together.

Without recriminations or judgments, they willingly stepped into the most challenging of problems innumerable times for Cambridge College as well as for me personally. A friend once called me the CVS of college presidents. I was accessible twenty-four hours a day, seven days a week. It was the same for Peggy Dulany, Elizabeth McCormack, Jon Larsen, and Anne Peretz who were engaged with me virtually around the clock. They were problem-solvers, networkers, and fund-raisers. Most of all, they helped me to endure.

In all the work that I was doing on behalf of the college, it was necessary to present myself as strong and confident, even though most of the time I actually felt vulnerable and anxious.

Through ongoing struggles with the faculty, struggles with regulatory agencies, and most of all with fundraising rejections, I often felt like the Shmoo character in the Li'l Abner comic strip, a spherical-shaped white blob with a big smile on its face. The other cartoon characters would punch and kick it until it fell over, but the Shmoo would bounce right back up with the same big smile ready for the next onslaught.

I lost many battles, but I never lost the war. My priority was to keep the college going no matter what, which meant that I had to find ways to keep myself going. I lived two different lives. My public life was filled with travel, meetings, decisions, and plans. Each day I worked until the clock ran out. Then I went home and collapsed.

I had great friends and some wonderful men in my life. And these people sustained me in my personal life, emotionally at least. My view on marriage never changed. It wasn't for me, and I have no regrets. I had relationships with men who cared about me, loved me even, but understood that I did not have much life left over for relationships. In reality, my idea of bliss was to send out for takeout, watch a basketball or football game, and go to bed. Even more so than in my earlier years in Philadelphia, it simply wasn't within me to meet the obligations that go along with intimate relationships or to find the energy to compromise. My own life and its pressures were about all I could manage.

With the help of this core group of trustees, I became stronger. My primary motivation was that the college needed strong leadership. I had to learn to cope. I couldn't afford to waste any energy feeling fearful and vulnerable. To become as effective as possible, I had to become more confident than was my nature. I had to learn not to take personally the endless rejections that I got when asking for money.

Fortunately, Peretz, as a trustee, dear friend, and trained therapist saw right through to my embattled spirit.

"You live like you have a secret, but you really don't." She once said to me.

Her remark provided an insight that unlocked for me one of the puzzles of my life. Although I had always functioned as a very competent professional, inside, I was still the fearful and awkward

With Anne Peretz, 1987.

eleven-year-old girl with the shaved head who was ashamed of my father's drinking. My constant worry was that the college might suffer because I wasn't always everything that I thought the college needed me to be.

Back then, it also helped that Anne, as the president of The Family Center in Somerville, the neighboring community to Cambridge, shared many of my professional and personal struggles. The Family Center had a mission parallel to that of Cambridge College—supporting inner-city families by providing services that built on their strengths and helping them reach their goals. As with the college, this approach ran against the mainstream orthodoxy and created opposition from established bureaucracies.

Anne and I raged against the prevailing power structures together. We laughed, we cried, we ranted and raved and got each other through some truly awful experiences.

Yet another of our trustees who was skilled in the art of problem solving and crisis management was K. Dun Gifford. As a teenager he had survived the sinking of the *Andrea Doria,* and later in life as a political aide, he managed crises at the center of two of America's most prominent families. He was at the side of Bobby Kennedy when Kennedy was murdered, and was with Ted Kennedy in the aftermath of Chappaquiddick. Gifford was the trustee we turned to when conventional solutions were out of reach.

Early on, in the late seventies, when the IOE had been struggling with significant cash flow problems, Gifford had found an innovative and daring way for us to stay afloat until we raised enough money in gifts and grants to supplement our tuition income. On behalf of the board, Gifford wrote to the retirement insurance provider, TIAA-CREF, informing them that the IOE would not be paying into the fund for the current fiscal year and reassuring the provider that the Institute would pay all liabilities with interest in subsequent years.

Time and time again, the courage, creativity and stature of our trustees enabled the College to find solutions to problems that seemed to defy solutions. Blenda Wilson's strategies for maneuvering with the Massachusetts Board of Higher Education, Peggy Dulany's father's intervention with the United States Department of Education for financial aid as well as Dun's bold announcement to TIAA-CREF were all examples of the kind of support from the trustees that allowed me to turn the dream of Cambridge College into a reality.

Chapter 15

"Having the most radical person in the institution be the president creates a very strange dynamic," a member of our administration once said during one of our many discussions on how to maintain the college's mission.

This was a funny, but true, statement; however, it would not have been possible without a commitment to shared values. Fortunately, the faculty and trustees believed, as I did, that the traditional markers of intellectual capacity were not adequate to measure a student's ability to learn and be successful, and so we continued to forge ahead.

By the end of the eighties, because of our track record in preparing minority teachers to become more effective in their classrooms, Cambridge College received an $880,000 grant from the Wallace Foundation to prepare 100 bilingual aides, teacher aides, and parent volunteers to become certified teachers.

The foundation had funded a total of forty-five colleges across the country with $39 million. At the end of the first round, they conducted rigorous evaluations, chose the four best, and funded them again. Cambridge College was one of the four.

The president of the Wallace Foundation asked me to come to New York City and address the original group of forty-five. I really was not looking forward to being a human dartboard for disappointed college presidents and deans who had not been re-funded. However, I was agreeably surprised to find that they really wanted to know how Cambridge College was able to be successful, especially how we kept our faculty from treating these students as second-class citizens.

It was not an easy question to answer; the value system, the learning model, and the faculty mix at Cambridge College made the notion of anyone as a second-class citizen completely anathema.

The major measure of an institution of higher learning is, in my view, its capacity to help its students journey through learning processes to graduate, at the exit, ready to assume leadership roles in their personal and professional lives.

The *Boston Globe* once captured the distinctiveness of Cambridge College in an editorial entitled "Second Chance School." While discussing the editorial with some of our students, one of them said to me that, "for most of us, it really is a first chance."

Through the years so many students have expressed to us time and time again what it felt like to be in a place where their essential selves were valued. Other educators, the media, foundations, and many others have often asked how we achieved that sense of community in such a diverse institution.

Ron Homer, when he served as a trustee, suggested that "the way the table is set is the way people sit down."

As simplistic as that sounds, that was the case. We had set a table at the college where all were welcome, all were accepted, and the experience of each was valued.

As a result, anything less than respect for each individual was unthinkable at Cambridge College. There was diversity at every level of the institution, and that organizational structure communicated inclusion. The students trusted what we said because we were living and working what we believed.

So widespread was the ownership of this culture of respect for the students that on the rare occasion that a student was disrespected in anyway by anyone, there was always someone—a faculty member, an administrator, another student, or even a trustee—to confront it.

In the early 1980s, Digital Equipment Corporation (DEC) had donated computers to the college and we appointed an adjunct faculty member to teach an introductory course. He considered himself a political radical and enjoyed the responses he received to his inflammatory comments, something everyone around him took in stride, including students. But he crossed a line one evening when he said that "DEC is a dirtier word than the N-word," using the racial epithet itself.

Several African-American women in his class had been uncomfortable, and went to another faculty member, who in turn came to me. I called the instructor immediately, telling him that his insensitivity to his students was a concern.

"If these women are too ignorant to understand what I was trying to say, they don't belong in college," he stated.

My response was swift and clear.

"Someone who considers our students ignorant because they were offended by an offensive word isn't the right person to be teaching at Cambridge College."

I told him he would be paid for the rest of the semester but would not be returning to the class.

As I was introducing his replacement to the class, he returned, shouting that I was "an authoritarian bitch."

I stepped back as he stepped toward me, and I tripped and fell. The students then chased him out of the building.

All of us, trustees and faculty, were radical in the sense that we would not permit our students to be disrespected. We were committed to making Cambridge College a safe space that provided our students with the opportunity to catch up on the educational background they may have been denied—and, if possible, a chance to heal spirits battered by the race, class, and gender struggles in which they had been engaged.

To me, the most important thing about a learning community is that it must be a place of love, a place of unconditional acceptance of and respect for each person's essential self.

No one knows better than the deeply wounded that love heals. To be Black in a white-dominated world, to be a woman in a culture where only the men matter, to speak English with an accent that marks the speaker as someone outside of the mainstream. Before learning can happen, the wounds must begin to heal. So many people have been taught that their very being is the wound, and those internal wounds only begin to heal when people start to value, and indeed to love, themselves.

People who come to Cambridge College—students, faculty, and administrators, but especially students—find themselves respected and valued. Not only are these the core values within our model, but they are the foundations of how we existed within the spaces in which we worked and learned together.

So many people have come to us never having had a place like this earlier in their lives—not at home, not at school, not anywhere. And without that place, their power and potential could not flourish. It is almost impossible to take the kind of risks necessary for real learning without first having a sense of feeling safe and valued. In order to learn, people must trust themselves and trust what they know; when those around them value them and trust their knowledge, the students come to believe in themselves and in what they know.

In creating Cambridge College, I imagined classrooms where adult learners drew on the wealth of their own life experiences as they engaged actively with a rich body of academic knowledge and relevant research. Our learning model was richly detailed and had a simple and elegant philosophy at its core: each of us has things to teach and things to learn, and none of us knows what all of us know.

Cambridge College has also been very fortunate in the composition of its faculty, which has mirrored the diversity of our students. All of the faculty have been scholar/practitioners who have been able to fulfill their professional roles as educators, therapists, and managers and to teach our students how to master the academic content and the skill sets to be successful in their fields. In addition to their teaching responsibilities, the faculty have helped us to present the learning model to other constituencies.

The notion of student-centered learning and peer teaching are best conveyed by demonstration, particularly to people skeptical of their efficacy. As a result, a class taught by a student or a faculty member was always an important fundraising tool. One of our faculty, Mahesh Sharma, who was an authority on the teaching of math to young children, was particularly effective in these presentations.

In 1987 we made a fund-raising trip to Chicago, where Sondra Epstein, a Chicago-based trustee hosted a group of foundation officials and individual donors for the purpose of showing the effect of the Cambridge College learning model in action. Sondra, the potential donors, Mahesh, and I took a bus to visit the lowest-performing school in one of the poorest Chicago neighborhoods.

Arrangements had been made for Mahesh to teach fractions to a third-grade class. After introducing himself to the class, he asked the students to push their desks into groups of four. He distributed pieces of paper, cut into strips, secured by a paper clip. Then he started the lesson asking that they fold the paper once and tell him how many sections there were. When they said, "Two," he elaborated on the concept of two halves making a whole.

The donors and I were sitting along the side of the classroom. I was sitting beside an official from the MacArthur Foundation, and we were observing the four children in the group in front of us. One little boy, named De Lawrence, was extremely excited. He was holding his little slips of paper like they were lumps of gold. But there was a little girl in this group who became quite bewildered as the exercise proceeded. Mahesh kept saying once you get it right; help the others in your group. When Mahesh got to folding the paper four times, the little girl was completely lost.

De Lawrence leaned across and said to her, "If you had a dollar, how many quarters would you have?"

When the little girl said "four," De Lawrence very solemnly explained, "See this isn't just about little pieces of paper; it's about everything."

The MacArthur official said, "Bring Cambridge College to Chicago and you can write your own ticket."

With Mahesh Sharma, 1980s.

He saw what everyone else did, and how much that lesson was enhanced by supporting each student's starting point; the students were learning by doing and they were learning from and teaching one another.

In addition to being gifted teacher, Mahesh had a great capacity for organization and leadership. He had come to us from a very different and distant culture, yet his core values were in many ways identical to those of our trustees, faculty, and staff. He was a well-respected mathematician with a deep sense of the power of knowledge and a profound commitment to sharing that belief with others.

Mahesh had become an adjunct faculty member in the education program at the IOE in 1973, and also worked with the Boston-based Education Development Corporation, a federally-funded curriculum development organization.

In 1986, he became a full-time faculty member at Cambridge College, and in 1988, he was appointed the dean of our School of Education.

His values, his commitment to our mission, and his considerable talents were clear. By this time, he was also internationally recognized as an authority on dyscalculia, the math learning disability analogous to dyslexia.

For the first time since Joan Goldsmith left in 1979, I had a partner again.

Together, Mahesh and I began to expand the scope of the college, to increase enrollment and add programs of all kinds.

In 1990, under Mahesh's leadership, we created a summer residency program for practicing teachers that we called NITE, the National Institute for Teaching Excellence.

In this, as with so many other elements of the college's growth, we harkened back to the original model of the IOE that had existed at Newton College—but without its dormitory resources. As a result, we rented a college campus each summer to house students, all practicing teachers seeking to improve their classroom performance. Renting campuses that were empty in the summer allowed us to avoid the high maintenance costs of a residential campus. One of our staff said we lived "on the guerilla." We foraged around for existing resources rather than taking on the expense of retaining our own.

As always, our lack of orthodoxy created zany moments. I went with the college's attorney to assess the suitability of Pine Manor College in Chestnut Hill, Massachusetts, for our summer campus. The president took us on a tour.

"Fine," I said, "we'll take it."

The president said, "Just have the man in charge come to sign the papers." Our startled attorney sputtered out, "Eileen is the man in charge."

But some of the incidents throughout the years were much more serious in nature. In the summer of 1998, when 500 of our NITE students were housed at Mt. Ida College in Newton, we experienced local racism.

A nighttime thunderstorm led to a power failure on the campus,

NITE program outdoor class.

and it was unsafe for the students, all adult teachers from schools across America, to sleep in the dormitories. The city of Newton worked efficiently with the college staff to get buses to take students to area motels.

The staff called each motel, explained the situation, and reserved the available rooms.

Mahesh Sharma, who also served as the director of the NITE program, gave the college's credit card number over the telephone and agreed to go to each motel to sign receipts once the students were settled.

When two busloads of predominately African-American students (60 percent of that year's NITE class was African-American) arrived at the Red Roof Inn in Framingham the manager locked the doors to the lobby, and told the students to line up outside.

He said he was unsure he had as many vacant rooms as he'd thought and said he needed a credit card before anyone would be allowed in. Incredibly, he referred an older woman with a cane to a bathroom across the highway at a fast-food restaurant. The students produced their own credit cards, but the manager continued to resist. One student called Mahesh, who told them to board the buses while he found other accommodations.

"Don't stay there," he said. "I'll find another place where you are welcome."

Our trustees, Mahesh, and I were all tempted to use this incident as a public relations nightmare for the "Red Neck Inn," as Jon Larsen dubbed the establishment. But we decided to conserve our resources for our mission.

The college sued the motel on behalf of the students and won a settlement for each wronged student, though that did nothing to assuage the pain they suffered. When I met with the students, several women and men from Mississippi, Alabama, and Georgia, talked about never having experienced this kind of racism firsthand.

"I had heard my parents and grandparents talk about the humiliation they had endured when they were growing up, but I had never been denied service because of my color," said one student. "I had no idea how soul-eroding it was until this happened to me."

The irony was not lost on any of us that students from the Deep South had come to the home of many of the original abolitionists to have their civil rights denied. The Greater Boston area may have been one of the few places in the country where such a blatant violation of a public accommodation act could have happened at the end of the twentieth century.

The students, however, had a good learning experience in the program itself.

At the end of the summer, I received a note from a white teacher from Georgia who had been in the NITE program. She said that a colleague had asked her what she had learned at Cambridge College.

"I touched the future this summer," she answered. "I went into teaching because I believed that education was the best hope for healing the wounds of race and for us to go forward together. I was very disappointed in my early days of teaching because I wasn't able to make this happen. This summer I lived that experience and learned how to make it real in my own classroom."

Chapter 16

As the demand for our programs grew, we continued to expand the reach of the college.

In 1991, the college received new degree authorization for a Master of Management degree, an important step in our development. Until that point all of our students, regardless of department, had received Master of Education degrees.

But even though we could now offer a Master of Management degree as well as a Master of Education degree, we knew that in order to provide opportunities to a larger population of students, we would ultimately need the authority to offer an undergraduate degree.

When we had started the IOE in 1971, our goal had been to help create equal educational opportunity for inner-city students by training the teachers, counselors, and administrators who worked in those schools. Over the years, as we grew into Cambridge College, it became clear that we were making an impact on two levels: our graduates were making a difference in their communities as teachers, social service workers, and managers, and we were also providing the "first door" to higher education for those to whom it had been limited or denied.

In our early days back at Newton College, we had started the practice of accepting students without a bachelor degree. Since then, we had continued to accept a small number of these students each year, but we had still been forced to turn away large numbers of non-degree students who needed more academic preparation to be successful at the College. It was especially hard to turn away those students who needed a BA to take the next step in their careers.

Getting baccalaureate authority was my biggest dream and also one that seemed completely out of reach.

In order to apply for authority, we would first have to design and implement a program. Then the Massachusetts Board of Higher Education and the New England Association of Schools and Colleges would visit and decide whether to grant the authority. There was no way to do any of this without significant new funding.

The trustees retained a consultant to undertake a feasibility study for a capital campaign to fund the development of a BA program and other growth needs for the college. The consultant strongly advised against launching such a campaign. He felt that the minimum goal for a campaign was $3 million, and in his professional opinion, that number was completely beyond our ability to achieve.

But we had learned that conventional wisdom often didn't seem to apply to Cambridge College. Necessity drove us forward. We set and met a goal of $15 million in three years.

Critical to our success in achieving these goals was another piece of extraordinary good fortune. At the time, a very wealthy man, Charles Feeney, was giving money anonymously to innovative programs that would allow disadvantaged people to improve their situations through their own efforts. The money was given through the Atlantic Philanthropic Service Company (APS), incorporated in Bermuda to preserve Feeney's anonymity. Through a Rockefeller family contact, I was introduced to the president of APS, Ray Handlan, whose job was to find programs that fulfilled this mission.

Ray's value system and commitment to social justice made him a perfect fit with Cambridge College. He came from a working-class background himself, and had been an outstanding student and star basketball player at Cornell University. He was a deeply moral man who had a belief in the nearly redemptive power of philanthropy,

Ray Handlan with his wife, Shar, 1990s.

making him the ideal person to fulfill the mission that Charles Feeney, the donor, had established.

Ray spent several months evaluating the college's efficacy, leadership, and distinctiveness, finding that the college *was* indeed accomplishing its mission, but wondered aloud if our students could have attended any college's evening program with the same result. I didn't think so, I told him. I suggested it would be important for him to evaluate this for himself.

After visiting and comparing several programs to ours, he reported back: "American higher education is where the American automobile industry was in the 1970s and Cambridge College is more like the Japanese auto industry: efficient and forward looking, a quality product at the right price."

APS suggested a challenge grant of $1.5 million to launch our $15 million campaign. But in order to qualify for the $1.5 million, we first had to raise $6 million from others. Ray Handlan joined Elizabeth McCormack in mentoring and coaching me while providing introductions to foundations and generous individuals. Peggy Dulany, Jon Larsen, and Anne Peretz all provided generous leadership gifts of their own, even as they continued to help me cultivate and solicit other donors.

As the culminating event in the challenge phase to raise the initial $6 million, Peggy hosted an event at Kykuit, the Rockefeller family estate in Pocantico Hills, N.Y. Bill Moyers moderated a panel of prominent educators on the topic of "Education for 21st Century Citizenship," which was followed by a dinner party for the one hundred foundation officials and wealthy individuals in attendance.

Jon Larsen circled the room during the cocktails, soliciting donors to help us reach our goal and constantly recalculating totals. Then he and Anne Peretz would pledge again themselves.

Then he would go around again because, of course, the closer to the goal, the more motivated donors are to want to close the gap.

Elizabeth McCormack, Bill Moyers, me, and Peggy Dulany at Pocantico, 1980s.

By the end of the evening, donors had contributed the additional $250,000 we needed to reach our $6 million goal, which qualified us for the $1.5 million challenge from APS. It was another stunning achievement and a great testimony to the commitment of our trustees.

At the same time that we were working toward being able to offer own BA program, we were also simultaneously searching for a building of our own as part of our campaign to expand and solidify the foundations of the college. We had always dreamed of owning a building of our own, but for years it had remained out of our reach.

Back in the early 1980s, I had asked a real estate agent to look for a small building that the college could buy that was close to the Harvard Graduate School of Education where our classroom and library space were located. The agent had found a school building on Brattle Street, just two blocks from the Harvard Ed School.

It had been a post-secondary school, New Prep, for rich kids needing an extra year of academic preparation in order for colleges to accept them. The building had four large, beautiful classrooms, several multi-purpose rooms, including an auditorium in the basement, and some office space. It was perfect for our needs.

At the time, several trustees willing to help with the financing joined me in a meeting with the owner. It all seemed possible. The school was in the same block as the Harvard Divinity School and a Seventh Day Adventist complex, but the block also included some private residences.

I had previously met the immediate neighbors at a cocktail party that one of our trustees had given for the college, so I called them to say that we were considering buying the school next door to their homes and hoped to meet and discuss our plans. We wanted to assure them that we intended to be very good neighbors. The New Prep students had been notorious for rowdy behavior. Our students were all adults who were very serious about their education.

The next day, I came home from a day of teaching, turned on my answering machine, and heard a woman's voice say, "You are not what we want in our back yard; Brattle Street is not *that kind of street*."

I was so stunned and unsettled that I called Elizabeth McCormack and sobbed in relaying the story. In an effort to calm me down, she said that the woman was not talking about me personally. I told her that if she didn't want me as a neighbor, it wouldn't bother me in the slightest. I wouldn't particularly want her as a neighbor. What upset me was that our students had been so categorically rejected.

My answering machine was soon flooded with phone calls from other Brattle Street residents. One caller suggested that perhaps she and some of her friends could help us raise money to buy a building somewhere other than in Cambridge.

Another asked, "Why would you want to go where you're not wanted?"

In my naiveté I responded, "This is America. You don't have to be wanted; you just have to pay the mortgage."

The president of the Cambridge Historical Society called saying he would oppose any changes to the building. I asked him if it was his practice to call every prospective buyer of every building with similar warnings.

A city councilor very supportive of the college asked me to understand that this was a residential neighborhood.

"This building is already a school," I said to him. "There are chalkboards on the walls, desks bolted to the floor, an auditorium in the basement. It could never be a residence; it would have to be torn down, which the historical society says it won't permit. I realize these Brattle Street neighbors are a major financial source for you. I don't expect you to go against them, but please don't insult my intelligence with the argument that the neighbors' objections have nothing to do with race and class."

It was clear that if we proceeded, we were in for a long, expensive, time-consuming battle. The trustees told me that it was my decision; they would go forward if I wanted to. After much reflection, I decided that it would be a major distraction, a diversion of significant resources at a time when we had none to spare. We didn't go forward; today the building is the Harvard Land Grant Institute.

Over the next ten years, we continued to hope that we could find an affordable and ideally located building. In the meantime, we rented more and more office and classroom space from Harvard around Harvard Square and in the surrounding neighborhoods. Renting was becoming prohibitively expensive, making it even harder to accumulate enough money to buy a building. We were still using all our resources to support the academic programs and to award scholarships.

Then, in September of 1991, just as we were expanding the college in other ways, Dan Rothenberg, a wealthy, smart, and socially committed real estate developer visited the college and made a generous gift. As he was leaving, he asked me how much rent we paid.

When I answered "$750,000," he said, "That is too much. Give me a call if you ever want to acquire a building of your own."

I called him the next morning, and he began the search for the perfect building. Over the next year, in-between our furious fundraising, he looked with us for a building that would meet our space needs. At first Dan did not realize that we had no money to buy a building, but that didn't stop me from looking, and from believing that it was in the college's best interests to have one.

From time to time, reality overwhelmed me and I would ask Dan, "What if we can't find enough money when the time comes?"

He always answered, "Don't worry."

With so many things to worry about; I took his advice. I would worry when the time came. Early in 1992, that time came. Dan had found the perfect building, at 1000 Massachusetts Avenue in Cambridge, halfway between the Harvard and M.I.T. campuses, and large enough to house our offices and our classrooms. It had been offered to us for $14 million. Dan negotiated for several months, bringing the price down to $10 million. Through all of this, I remained hopeful that we would find the money we needed when the time came.

On a Friday morning in April, Dan called and said, "The college will need to make a down payment of $1 million. Can you do that by next Friday?"

I was flabbergasted. "Dan," I said, "remember when I asked you how much money we would need and you told me not to worry?"

There was an awkward pause, and I sensed genuine worry coming now from the other side of the line.

"You can't buy a $10 million dollar building," he said, "if you don't even have $1 million." Now I had to reassure him that his efforts had not been in vain.

"Of course, you're right," I said, knowing how vague this sounded. "May I get back to you this afternoon?"

I immediately called the three trustees who could possibly produce $1 million in a week, Peggy Dulany, Anne Peretz, and Jonathan Larsen.

Peggy and Anne were both out of the country. I called all the numbers I had for Jon and found him at a number that I had never used before. It felt like magic to have him materialize just as I was running out of hope.

When he answered, I explained the situation and asked the question, "Can we find $1 million by next Friday?"

"Say yes to Dan, and we'll find a way to make it come true," Jon said.

The next seven days were a frantic race to the finish. We had come a long way from that day twenty-one years before when Joan Goldsmith and I had spent our last $46 on a taxi to IBM headquarters looking for $50,000 from Tom Horton and Vin Learson. But I was still in a high stakes gamble to make the dream of Cambridge College come true. This time I needed a million dollars, not $50,000—and this time Cambridge College had quite a few more friends and donors than it had had in 1972.

By the end of that nerve wracking week, four friends had come through for us, exhibiting generosity—$250,000 each—that moves me to this day.

Although we had raised the down payment, Dan Rothenberg realized that he was securing a building for a college that really couldn't afford to pay for it.

He and I were walking back from a meeting at 1000 Massachusetts Avenue, and he stopped, looked me straight in the eye, and said, "*Now* I understand how you created the college. If I had seen it clearly at the start, I'm not certain what I would have done, but I will see this through with you." And he took my hand.

Through Dan's expert negotiation, we secured the building for $7.5 million. With a challenge grant from the Kresge Foundation and the generosity of our trustees, we raised the money we needed.

In February 1994, Cambridge College moved into its new home, a modern, spacious, and solid four-story brick building with enough rental space to bring the college one million dollars a year in income to pay our overhead and fund some scholarships. Our location, halfway between Harvard and MIT, seemed to many of us a splendid symbolic bonus.

Our BA program also began that same year, and through our fundraising efforts we had raised enough to fund scholarships for our neediest students.

My worries were not over, but I knew then that our mission would carry on, that Cambridge College was now an institution that would outlive me and continue to create lasting change in all the lives it touched.

Chapter 17

In February 1994, Cambridge College started a new chapter in its institutional history with the ownership of our own building. On the day renovations were completed, the first day of the new semester, the entire faculty, staff, and I walked the short distance from our rented space in Harvard Square to 1000 Massachusetts Ave.

As we entered, I was overwhelmed with emotion at the sight of our splendid new space and with the realization of what it meant for our future. As the students began to arrive, it was clear that they too experienced a new sense of belonging in a home of their own.

I had spent every waking moment of the two decades leading up to that moment worrying about how to take the college from one fiscal year to the next. Now Cambridge College was in a "new place" in every sense of the expression, but we still had long-term financial needs that were not going to be met by our tuition-based income and rental income from our building. Unlike the majority of private educational institutions, we did not yet have an endowment; however, neither did we have the expenses of a large residential campus to maintain.

Because we had the luxury of many trustees willing to provide legal, financial, and real estate knowledge and experience, we had always been able to keep our administration lean and our resources focused on instruction. Unlike many educational institutions, public and private, we were committed to keeping our tuition and costs

1000 Massachusetts Avenue.

Dedication of the Dulany Atrium. (Left to right) Dan Rothenberg, me, David Rockefeller and Jonathan Larsen.

as affordable as possible, not raising the cost of attending the college annually at two and three times the rate of inflation, as many institutions do routinely. Having a building of our own provided the College with a solid foundation; however, there were many problems yet to be resolved.

I have always focused on what worked and hoped for the best with what didn't. I could find a silver lining in a tornado funnel. For the first thirty years or so of the institution's history, positive energy had carried the day. All the problems—not enough money, too few people doing too many jobs, not enough infrastructure to support a rapidly growing institution—increased with the growth of the college.

As a result, there was an almost Wizard of Oz quality to our lives; every day we made everything work for that day, but it was very important not to look behind the curtain. There was constant concern and tension among the faculty, staff, and administration, but everyone agreed that as hard as it was to make Cambridge College work, it always worked for the students. And for all of us that is what mattered the most.

Through all the challenges, and despite our differences, the trustees, faculty, and I had all worked toward the same goals together. We had done it well and every day there were problems—some that had to be solved that day, some that required solutions that would take months of energy and resources, and some that we weren't sure could ever be solved. But we worked on all of them together with good will, hope, and perhaps more than a little delusion.

The narrative always was, "We will find a way." To quote Jon Larsen when I asked him if we could find a million dollars in a week's time for a down payment on 1000 Massachusetts Avenue: "Say yes and we will find a way to make it come true." Jon's reply became our mantra.

In looking back over my years at Cambridge College, I realize that even the story of the early years looks easier and happier than it actually was living it at the time. It was never so straightforward and linear. But no matter what happened, we had just kept creating possibility and allowing will to triumph over reality.

Over the years, the founding trustees had found a way to achieve seemingly impossible goals. Together we had almost miraculously found a way to gain access to federal financial aid for our students, to buy a building even though we lacked the money for a down payment, and to face so many other challenging situations.

Now that these basic challenges had been met, the issues facing us became more amorphous. The fundamental challenge was that as the college grew, it became difficult to sustain the level of change to which we were committed.

Everyone was proud that Cambridge College was the most diverse college in New England. For several years the college had awarded more masters degrees to African-American students than any college in the country. Our immigrant population was just as distinctive; we were fourth in the nation in awarding masters degrees to Hispanics and we were the only college in New England with a statistically significant number of Vietnamese, Laotian, and Cambodian students.

At a rhetorical level, everyone valued this diversity and espoused support for the mission; however some new trustees, as well as officers within the regulatory agencies and certain funders, were beginning to demand that we find ways to prove that our students were comparable to students at other colleges.

For our first thirty years, the founding trustees had understood that living out our mission required courage and commitment. But now we had some trustees who wanted it both ways. They wanted, or thought they wanted, diversity and inclusiveness; but they also wanted proof that our students were as good as students who could pass through the gate at more traditional colleges, those with high SAT scores and acceptable high school grade point averages.

Just as I had learned in Philadelphia, it was clear that the rhetorical commitment to change was quite different from actual commitment to change. The belief on the part of so many people that "different is less than" prevails against all evidence to the contrary.

Banner in the college cafeteria.

In the mid-nineties, two books dramatized this fundamental issue. *The Bell Curve: Intelligence and Class Structure in American Life* by Charles Murray and Richard Herrnstein, purported to examine the bell-shaped normal distribution of intelligence quotient. Murray and Herrnstein concluded that, "It seems highly likely to us that both genes and the environment have something to do with racial differences." This book became the gospel for everyone who had a stake in resisting affirmative action and increased diversity in higher education. Murray and the book itself were discussed in all the major publications. Herrnstein died before the book was published, but Murray appeared on what seemed like a daily basis for months on every television and radio program. New books were written expanding on this premise.

Several years later, Derek Bok, the former president of Harvard, and William Bowen, the former president of Princeton, wrote, *The Shape of the River: Long-Term Consequences of Considering Race in College and University Admissions*. Using the files of forty-five thousand students of all races who attended academically selective colleges between the 1970s and early 1990s the book provides the empirical support to demonstrate that, "given the opportunity, minority students do as well or better than white counterparts at the nation's top universities on a number of educational outcomes." Despite having been written by two of the country's most prominent educators, this book was largely ignored. It received very little press coverage and there were very few media outlets that featured appearances by Bok and Bowen to discuss it.

If these two distinguished scholars who had national stature in educational matters could not convince people who were skeptical of the educability of all students, despite their race or ethnicity, I realized that it was futile for me to try. Nevertheless, I did try.

There were constant questions about the implications for the quality of the college when there were so many more African-American or Hispanic students than there were at other liberal arts colleges. The very offensive question of whether the diversity of our students meant that Cambridge College was a diploma mill began to be a concern for this group. For me this diploma mill discussion was absolutely maddening.

Ours were hard-working students, who sacrificed family or work time to attend nightly classes and weekend sessions. Many came from economically hard-hit inner cities and many were teaching children in low-performing urban schools, counseling people in need at community organizations, or seeking improvement in their skills in order to advance in their management careers. Degrees were earned, not mailed when checks arrived, the classic definition of a diploma mill.

Our student population was not the profile of the children of the upper- and middle-classes attending Ivy League or other elite liberal arts colleges; but our students *were* every bit the profile of the people who built America, those who sought education to improve their knowledge as a means to build careers and strove to build stronger financial security and better lives for themselves and their children.

Given the dismal performance of inner-city public schools, it was impossible to judge a student's potential through high school records alone. It was also well documented, even by the administrators of the College Board, that there was no correlation between high SAT scores and success after college. The concern had to be about the learning experience of the students in the course work that they were taking at the college.

Our emphasis on a student's ability to develop in his or her own chosen career was not unlike any other college or university that prepared its students for their futures. The urgency for our students was that they were in the workplace right then, helping teachers, teaching in low performing public schools, counseling in agencies and serving in other capacities for institutions so important to their communities. We were a career-focused institution, not a vocational or technical school, but a college where people already committed to their careers learned how to better perform and to earn the credentials that will help them advance in their careers.

Among our graduates, there were significant numbers of paraprofessionals who became teachers, teachers who became principals and superintendents, counselors who became heads of agencies, entry-level workers who became managers. Ideally, we would have had the resources to document all of the success stories. But instead of using precious resources to catalog and promote the success of our graduates or promote ourselves, we invested the bulk of our resources in the futures of our students and the prospective students knocking on our door.

There is a line that is attributed to the comedian Martin Mull: "Writing about music is like dancing about architecture." That is exactly how I feel when I try to persuade a skeptical person how and why the Cambridge College learning model works. It is really one of those things that you either get it or you don't. You either believe that everyone has the capacity to learn or not.

As Archibald MacLeish said, "It is not in the world of ideas that life is lived. Life is lived, for better or worse, in life." Adults who have not had the opportunity for higher education have nonetheless

Celtics legend Bill Russell delivered the commencement address at Cambridge College's 34th Commencement in 2005. Russell was also presented an honorary Doctor of Humane Letters degree.

learned a great deal from their lives, their peers, and their work experience.

At Cambridge College we were helping students to acknowledge and trust what they knew already and then providing the curriculum to build on that learning. We were helping our students connect the world of ideas to their lives and careers, and the theory/practice interplay was very powerful. Students were learning not only from the faculty and their textbooks but from their peers, from their jobs, and from the people whom they are teaching, counseling or managing.

With prospective funders, I tried to demonstrate the college's learning model through presentations by students and alumni about the impact of their experiences at the college on their lives and careers.

A fairly typical example of this was a meeting I had with a foundation funder where I introduced him to a young Hispanic man who worked for the Commonwealth of Massachusetts, designing and conducting workshops in Spanish for non-English speakers who had been convicted of drunk driving offenses.

This student talked about his realization that the powerlessness these offenders felt in their lives contributed to their drinking problems. As a result of this realization, he spent some time at the beginning of the several-week sessions talking with them about their lives, particularly their work lives. He created a curriculum to help them learn the English words to express their rights as laborers and present their grievances appropriately.

The student talked about the powerful transformative effect this approach had in his groups. He had the lowest recidivism rates of any of the instructors leading these sessions and had been promoted and was now training other workshop leaders. This kind of outcome, which resulted in a student incorporating his own life experience into the college's curriculum and creating a result that someone relying on academic knowledge alone might not have discovered, was at the heart of the Cambridge College learning model.

The prospective funder was very skeptical and said "Yes, but what academic content did you learn?"

The student said, "I learned that people who feel powerless need to learn how to gain some control in their lives in order to stop sabotaging themselves with alcohol and drugs."

Realizing that that wasn't real learning as far as the funder was concerned, I asked the student, "Did you read *The Pedagogy of the Oppressed* by Paolo Freire in your humanities class?"

He said, "Yes, that's what gave me the idea."

The student had taken Freire's theory and put it directly into practice.

Interestingly enough, Paolo Freire had actually given a presentation at the Harvard Graduate School of Education while I had been there as a student. Part of my enjoyment of his presentation had come from his refusal to speak English, thereby letting people grope along as well as they could, much as non-English speakers must do every day. In the days and weeks following his appearance, the Ed School students endlessly parsed his theories; however, I'm not certain how many of them could have adapted those theories into practice as our student had.

With Cambridge College, it had never been my intention to create a "good" liberal arts college in the traditional sense of the word. In my opinion the world didn't need another third-tier version of Harvard or Amherst. Contrary to the opinion of the woman who said many years ago in the college's early accreditation stages that I was seeking entry into the privileged club that higher education often resembles in its hierarchy, infrastructure and exclusivity, nothing was further from my objective.

What had driven me for thirty years was my hope and belief that there was a new day coming when the hierarchy of the club of higher education would be greatly expanded and profoundly more inclusive. Unfortunately, that was not the case.

The founding trustees, the faculty, and our early funders had well understood they were part of an enterprise that went against the prevailing orthodoxy. They understood too that it was essential that everyone providing leadership for the college operate out of the same value system and be prepared to answer the kinds of questions that invariably come up in an alternative institution.

But now, even though we had accomplished so much in expanding our programs and owning our own building, more and more time was being spent justifying the work of the college and its mission to people within the institution.

Chapter 18

In the late 1990s, around the same time as the "Red Neck Inn" incident, a small group of trustees, some funders, and some of the officials in regulatory agencies began to feel that the answer to the challenge of how to maintain the mission, achieve the same results, and still be more like other colleges was to find a traditional educator to be provost.

Throughout the history of the college, many of the faculty and staff, some of whom were Cambridge College graduates themselves, had become part of our community. Some longtime faculty and staff became administrators. As new faculty, staff, and trustees were added, they were absorbed into the existing culture, and they were proud to support the students and carry out the mission.

However, bringing someone in from another institution to provide leadership at the level of provost was very problematic and had been since Joan Goldsmith's departure in 1979.

There were few alternative institutions like ours. Even if qualified educators shared our mission, had they worked in a setting like ours? Did they share not only our vision, but our work ethic? Were they risk takers capable of courageous actions in difficult situations? Were they sufficiently confident in their knowledge and values and able to advance the institution even with the inevitable skepticism of their more traditional peers in higher education?

During the first search for a provost in 1980, Don Davies, a trustee very familiar with many of those holding leadership positions in higher education, had defined the search vividly, "We must find someone who is willing to carry his own yellow pad." That comment was prescient, as was true with so many of the observations of the trustees engaged in building the college.

In the twenty years that had followed, four senior executives had come and left; each had been more comfortable presiding over a college with all the trappings normally associated with the role than with the hard work of creating the future for an alternative institution that challenged many norms. There had been endless struggles, both substantive and cultural. Structurally, there was always a push to establish entrance requirements, to increase the tuition so that we could increase the number of administrators and support staff, and to put an emphasis on scholarly research.

On the cultural side were the vestiges of covert and often unconscious racism that would come to the surface under pressure. For example, one provost once chided an African-American faculty member for coming to a meeting on "CP time." After the ensuing uproar, the provost explained to me that at his last institution referring to "colored people's time" was just a joke and that no one had been offended. I told him that no joke about anyone's ethnicity was ever appropriate at Cambridge College; however, the damage was already done and so was he.

These cultural differences also manifested themselves in other ways, some around race and class, some about just adhering to the prerogatives of what it meant to be a college administrator. For instance, the man who was provost in 1998 was on his annual fishing trip during the "Red Neck Inn" fiasco. No amount of persuasion could convince him that observing his tradition of taking a month-long trip immediately after commencement was not appropriate in a college with a significant and complex summer program.

As this provost left in the summer of 1999, the college was faced with the prospect of yet another national search for the right person. By this time the group of trustees and funders who wanted to maintain the mission but become more like other colleges was stronger and more vocal.

It was August. The summer program was over, and it was the annual three-week period when a vacation was possible. I was renting a cottage on Chappaquiddick and I was sitting on the floor talking on a telephone that never stopped ringing when my friend, Bobbi Carrey, came to stay with me. When she tried to persuade me to at least move to a chair, I told her I was too anxious to even stand up. Bobbi joined me on the floor and I told her I couldn't go through it all again. I had gone past the point of I didn't want to, I had arrived at "I can't."

I made the decision to call the trustees and tell them that I was going to retire in a year. We would search for a new president. When we found the right person, I would remain through a transition period and then leave the college. It was the most amazingly liberating decision. I felt like someone I loved very much had died and left me an island in the Bahamas. I had such deep feelings of loss and grief mixed up with an exhilarating sense of freedom.

Throughout my life at the college, I had felt driven to do what was needed to be done to sustain the institution. As difficult and exhausting as that was, I was doing it as part of a small group of people working together. By 1999, there were many more variables at play.

In addition to the differences about the interpretation of the mission, there were several trustees and funders who had very mixed feelings about me personally.

One trustee summed it up by saying, "I think you are a great person. I just wish you were different."

It didn't help that in a way this was the message that I experienced as a child from my mother, my relatives, the nuns, and just about everyone in that small town where conforming to the norm was expected.

I think that anyone in a leadership position is the object of a significant amount of ambivalence. Most leaders deal with it. I, on the other hand, was uniquely unsuited for dealing with it. I felt enmeshed and suffocated by the engulfing ambivalence that was directed at me. My life didn't belong to me. I lived every day trying to convince, to please, to placate the trustees and funders who took issue with everything about me from my personal choices to my determination to maintain open admissions for our students.

I had justified for the last time why some students not speaking standard English or why the rumor that a student had plagiarized was not a reason to change the mission. I had arrived at the point that I simply could not do it any longer. I moved to a chair on the deck of the house I was renting and I began to call trustees to tell them about my decision.

I had an astonishing set of conversations; all of them quite supportive.

I realized that in my exhaustion and overwhelm, I had not really been defending myself against or sharing the scope of the negativity that was being directed toward me by a relatively small group of people.

It was my style to put the best face on things. I worried about bothering trustees, like Jonathan Larsen and Anne Peretz, who had helped me solve so many problems. I was worried too that by sharing my anxiety, I might contribute to a split on the board that had already begun to develop. Once I talked with them and with others, I realized what I should have known all along. This was not my problem to solve alone.

Bobbi observed that I was like someone in an abusive relationship. I had accepted so much inappropriate behavior from this small group of people that I was colluding in my own victimization. I had really re-created the circumstance of my childhood. No matter how hard I tried, no matter how much I did, I ended up feeling there was something fundamentally wrong with me.

In the hours and hours of telephone conversations that took place during the next three weeks, it was possible for me with key trustees and others at the college to reframe the narrative about the future of the college. It was not about me. It was about how to maintain the mission of providing educational opportunities for students of limited means when we had so few resources of our own.

If we were to maintain our commitment to not having a gate at the beginning for the students, we had to be able to provide adequate remediation. This meant that we had to generate more revenue from sources other than tuition or building income. We had to do much more fundraising.

As a result, the trustees and I made two important decisions. We would launch a $50 million capital campaign so that we could support better the learning needs of our students. And for the selection of a provost, we decided to build on our own strengths and promote an internal leader, Mahesh Sharma, who had been serving as dean of our School of Education for the last six years.

Jon Larsen, always offering a distinctive perspective, observed that our repeated attempts to bring in a traditional educator as second-in-command was analogous to organ transplants. It is not uncommon for patients to reject the "foreign body," even one intended to help.

Mahesh Sharma became provost in 1999 and continued working with me to provide the leadership for the college and to help create its future.

For years now he had shared my commitment and passion for the mission.

His worldview, like mine, had been shaped by the time and circumstances of his childhood. Born when India was still "the jewel in the British Crown," Mahesh had come of age during the time of Indian independence from the British Empire. A member of the Brahmin class, he was influenced both by his Anglophile grandfather and his revolutionary father. Coming to America to teach, he experienced many of the slights and indignities that befall new immigrants. He had, as I do, a deep sense of what it means to live the dual life of an insider and outsider. His commitment to our students and their ability to learn was profound.

Extremely driven and very entrepreneurial, Mahesh was largely responsible for the significant growth of the college over the next four years.

Our National Institute for Teaching Excellence expanded greatly after Mahesh became provost. It was the only program of its kind in the country and it served students from thirty-seven states and six countries, who all came to the greater Boston area to participate in it.

Originally, the NITE program had been designed as a masters degree completion program for practicing teachers who had completed most of their graduate courses at other institutions but needed to do the additional coursework and write a thesis to earn their degrees. But over the years, many prospective students had applied who needed additional coursework before they could qualify for the NITE program.

As we had done since the college had begun, we created a solution that responded to the needs of our students. We began offering additional courses in Georgia to accommodate those who wanted to apply to the NITE program but did not yet have enough coursework completed to do so. In earlier years, we had opened two additional Massachusetts campuses in Springfield in the mid-70s, and Lawrence in the 1990s; these additional NITE program courses in Georgia were the beginning of what became our first out-of-state campus, located in Augusta, Georgia.

Under Mahesh's leadership the college continued to expand in other ways. To better serve the theory/practice interplay that was at the heart of the Cambridge College learning model, we went on to establish collaborations with 170 schools, agencies businesses and organizations.

In the midst of all the growth and success, the conflicts that had begun to emerge in 1999 were still in play. We had a small group of trustees who always knew what they were against but never seemed to be for anything. Every problem was treated as if we were the only college that had ever had a problem.

Many of our collaborations were with agencies that served people who had transcended some of life's most difficult problems. People such as Ben Thompson, the graduate who had been a former convict himself who later became the Penal Commissioner for

Banner welcoming students to the NITE program, early 2000s.

the Commonwealth of Massachusetts. Thompson had become the Director of Strive, an organization designed to support former convicts to get an education and become gainfully employed, and some of those former convicts had enrolled in Cambridge College.

It was a concern for some of these trustees that one of these students might someday reflect poorly on the college.

In response, Jon Larsen observed that the "Unabomber" had graduated from Harvard and he had never heard anyone worry that Harvard might become known for its bomb making. As with all of Jon's observations, this was particularly apt. When a student or graduate of a traditional institution gets into trouble, building bombs or plagiarizing an essay, it is about the person. No one condemns the institution.

This conversation has always reminded me of the fear that my Black friends and students had when Kennedy was assassinated. Their first reaction was concern that if a Black person was responsible, the entire race would be condemned. I had been stunned by that reaction, but sadly had to realize it was true.

Mahesh and I, as well as many of the trustees, responded to these issues as they arose; but they were never resolved.

We struggled constantly to achieve the balance necessary to grow the College.

Cambridge College had always been a place where we found it easier to ask forgiveness than permission. We used this strategy with the regulatory agencies, though we always did so with the support of the trustees.

But as much as I had pushed against the boundaries of traditional education, Mahesh always wanted to push a little further, grow faster, start more programs.

Chapter 19

In 2003, after having been very effective as provost, Mahesh Sharma was appointed as the president of Cambridge College, and I became the chancellor.

In his role as president, Mahesh was responsible for the leadership of the college, and he reported directly to the board. As chancellor, my responsibilities were external; fundraising, public relations, and relations with the board of trustees, to whom I also reported. One major initiative of mine as chancellor was the establishment of an endowment, which would generate additional income for the college.

Once Mahesh became president, he had many struggles with the board. In his defense, he knew, as I did, that we were still trying to build an institution that would sustain itself into the future and we were doing it without the significant resources that traditional colleges have like endowments and real estate holdings.

In addition, key members of the original board had moved to emeritus status as Life Trustees. This left a leadership vacuum of individuals willing to leverage their own very considerable resources for the growth and development of the college, including helping the college raise millions of dollars for programs, student scholarships and its permanent home at 1000 Massachusetts Avenue.

The founding trustees and I had been very clear that we were creating a college with limited financial resources for people with limited financial resources themselves—which is why they had worked in concert with the college's leadership to problem-solve, creating solutions for nearly insolvable challenges for almost thirty years.

The newer trustees began to expect Mahesh and me to solve all the college's problems ourselves, but to do so in a manner that also met with their approval.

Mahesh was highly effective in the creation of new program offerings and new campuses; however, after he became president, he did not work as closely as needed with the board.

As president, he began to manage the college as he might have managed his own business, pushing the boundaries beyond reasonable limits. He weighed the risks of his decisions, took actions without board approval and sought ways to smooth things over when something did not work as expected.

Although the trustees and I were aware of this pattern and worked hard to convince Mahesh that this operating style was unacceptable and unsustainable, he continued to launch new initiatives without the appropriate college approvals.

Knowledge of new initiatives began to emerge about which the trustees and I were completely unaware, such as an unauthorized campus of Cambridge College in Mumbai, India.

In early December 2007, as the trustees and I were in the process of sorting out these actions and their resulting financial impact, someone in the college's accounting office anonymously sent documents to *The Boston Globe*. The newspaper published an article that included information which accelerated the trustee review and investigation that was already underway.

In January 2008, Mahesh Sharma resigned from Cambridge College.

Following Mahesh's resignation, the trustees asked me to become interim president as well as remaining as chancellor. I returned to the day-to-day management of the college and also began working with the accounting firm that the trustees had retained to identify any malfeasance or incompetence and to restore the credibility of our policies and procedures.

As interim president, I re-entered a changed institution.

misappropriated from the college, there were many accounting improprieties—i.e., using restricted funds for operations, allocating unfunded line items for bad debts and other accounts, and expenses that had not been booked.

As chancellor, my responsibilities had been external fundraising as well as board and public relations. I had not been responsible for the day-to-day operations and oversight of the college during the five years that Mahesh had been president. I don't mean that as an excuse. I should have known what was going on, the finance committee of the board should have known, the auditors should have known. We all should have known.

It was, however, a complex situation. It took six months for the accounting firm hired by the trustees to sort out the college's actual financial situation.

In July 2008, it became clear that in order to continue operations, in fact, even to meet the August payroll, the college would need to extend its $5 million credit line by an additional $6 million. This would require trustee action, and intervention, and several trustees stepped up.

Gerald Chertavian, chair of the board finance committee, Derek Davis, chair of board audit committee, and I met with the Cambridge Trust Company on July 30, 2008, to discuss extending the credit line to $11 million using our mortgage-free building at 1000 Massachusetts Avenue as collateral.

Although we knew that this was going to be a difficult meeting, we were completely unprepared for what happened.

Gerald, Derek, and I explained that this was a serious situation: the $5 million credit line had been spent down and the college did not have the resources to meet the August payroll. In order to fulfill our financial obligations going forward, we would need to secure an $11 million line of credit by the end of July.

We felt that although we had a problem, we also had the solution. We could leverage our building at 1000 Massachusetts Avenue, which had been appraised for $34 million and was unencumbered by

Life presents us very few cases where reality outdistances our dreams. But the reality of what Cambridge College had become exceeded my most ambitious aspirations.

In founding the IOE in 1971 with one hundred students, six full-time and four part-time faculty, and one degree offering on one campus as an affiliate of an existing college, I had dared to dream of an institution that represented the racial, ethnic, linguistic, economic, and generational diversity of urban America. One that drew on this diversity as a source of power, strength, and additional learning for all within its real and virtual walls.

Thirty-six years later Cambridge College was a fully accredited educational institution with an enrollment of 7,546 students, 1,146 faculty and six degree offerings including a Doctorate in Education, at our main campus in Cambridge. In addition, there were seven regional centers in four states, as well as in Puerto Rico.

It was beyond anything that I had imagined at the start, and the college was still growing.

The college's success was a direct result of the need for its programs and its mission within the broader society. For many of our students, we were their only option, the only affordable and relevant choice for their busy lives, a choice that valued them for who they were and what they had already learned in life.

But success had brought a new set of challenges; a larger college and a greater number of students required a larger infrastructure, better governance, and greater resources.

In responding to these challenges, the college needed the kinds of trustees who had "founded the college." For nearly thirty years, those original trustees and I had believed that we were doing something important and something very difficult to do: building a new learning model for those left out of higher education. But now, many of the founding trustees were in emeritus status, and the college needed a new set of miracles.

First and foremost, there was a financial crisis.

Although I don't believe that any money was actually

any mortgage. However, the officers at Cambridge Trust Company did not see themselves as part of the solution. They were angry that the college was in this position and that the bank itself was possibly in some jeopardy if we were not able to repay the line of credit.

They told us that they could not extend the credit line without another bank as a partner.

Moreover, a transaction involving a mortgage could not be completed in time for us to meet the August payroll.

After recovering from our profound shock, Gerald, Derek, and I began to frantically brainstorm ways to find an $11 million loan against our building within a seemingly impossible thirty days. Both Gerald and Derek were problem-solvers. Gerald had founded an important and thriving nonprofit, Year Up; and Derek Davis was a real estate attorney who specialized in complex projects.

We called Jon Larsen, who fortunately was not only still on the board, but also was now the chair of the board, to let him know that the situation was more dire than we had expected. As always, he stood ready to do whatever he could. He offered to extend a loan to the college for the more than half a million dollars needed to allow the college to meet the August payroll. Although this generous offer would allow us to avoid immediate disaster, it was not a solution to the larger problem.

Despite the fact that it was a Friday evening in July, Derek and I went directly to my house, where Derek started calling bankers he knew from his real estate dealings. Once again, the good fortune that had always been with Cambridge College was with us. Derek reached a senior officer at Century Bank who offered to meet with us. Fortunately for us, the bank had been founded by a man who had a lifelong commitment to social justice, Marshall Sloane.

Marshall had been born in working-class Somerville, where he had started a full-service commercial community bank whose focus was and remains providing financial services to small and medium sized businesses.

If our request for a loan had made no economic sense to the

bank, it wouldn't have happened. But our mission also appealed to Marshall, a man who remembered where he came from: his father was an immigrant, and the values embraced by Cambridge College were his own.

Marshall, and his two sons and daughter who served as officers of the bank, agreed to the loan, and worked with us every step of the way: We received the loan and made the August payroll.

Once again, a trustee had made a heroic effort to accomplish what was seemingly impossible.

Derek Davis, much like Peggy Dulany, Blenda Wilson, Jon Larsen and others before him, had saved the day.

Over the years, the trustees and I had been working toward what we facetiously called "a tidier world," our shorthand for the time when the college would have all the necessary internal mechanisms and practices firmly in place—when the college itself would run, as most colleges do, on a version of automatic pilot with an infrastructure that kept pace with growth, an endowment that provided a financial cushion and with ancillary support staff in marketing and other areas.

That "tidier world" had definitely not been realized as of 2008. We were still operating like a startup: our infrastructure was flat and lean, all our resources were devoted to providing an education to as many students as possible, and our administrative practices were still evolving, perhaps too slowly.

Most importantly, we had hoped that by now we would be operating in a world in which our mission was valued to the extent that financial support would be easier to generate, accreditation would not be a constant battle, and our students would be accepted as the qualified and truly extraordinary people they are, both before and after their Cambridge College experience.

It was our hope that we would have less of a need for the kinds of heroic and extraordinary efforts that had always been required of some of our trustees. However, that time had not yet come, and many of the trustees—particularly the ones who had not been part of the solution, had become weary of the struggle.

As long as the center held at the college—as long as the leadership and trustees continued to wage uphill battles around our distinctive mission and even more distinctive culture—the mission was preserved and enhanced.

However, the kind of prolonged struggle in which the college had been engaged—the struggle to resolve the crisis at hand while continuing to work to create the future—is exhausting. Mustering the positive energy to move forward takes more effort than falling back into negative energy. When you are involved in an enterprise that is struggling to change the status quo, you can't struggle among yourselves.

My approach has always been similar to that of Steve Jobs, the founder of Apple. The best way to predict the future, he said, is to create it. But that approach requires that everyone involved is creating it together. And for many years, despite the tensions it caused, that is what we had been doing: creating the future together, trusting that all decisions, even ones that turned out badly, were made in good faith and in the perceived best interest of the college.

As soon as the financial crisis was resolved, the search for the new president got underway. There was a core group of trustees who very much wanted that "tidier world" immediately, and pushed for "a fresh start".

My hope had been that the trustees and I would work together to find a new president who would have the courage, commitment, skill and work ethic to sustain the mission. The trustees who made up the search committee wanted a new president who believed in the mission, but perhaps in a more traditional way.

The question as the search moved forward was to what extent a new president would be willing to push constantly with all constituencies and against all odds to remain true to the mission. It was a question that haunted me; I'm not sure the search committee thought about it at all.

Instead of embracing the complexities that the college faced and working to resolve them, some of the trustees focused on where to place the blame for what had happened. And I became the target.

I have never found it helpful to think about blame. Negative energy is toxic; it drives out positive energy. It is exhausting to deal with and it was not possible to tackle the challenges that the college was facing, and had always faced, while fighting from within. There were certainly trustees who were committed to my vision and my leadership, but in any situation the people with the biggest investment of time and energy always prevail.

The issue wasn't whether I would remain as chancellor and interim president for the long-term. Under no circumstances would that have been desirable or possible. I had been in charge in one form or another for close to forty years. I was ready for peace. However, I wanted to be certain that the important work of the college would continue.

I did not want a repeat of what had happened at Antioch, decades of innovative success wiped out because the incoming president did not have the value system, the temperament, the work ethic or the skill to provide the leadership that the institution needed.

My hope was that the trustees would spend the time and energy to find the right president and that the college would make a thoughtful transition to the future. However, the prevailing wisdom became that I should leave as soon as possible, and that the new president should not "live in my shadow."

The six months between the time these decisions were made in October 2008, until the new president was appointed on March 1, 2009, were extraordinarily difficult for me.

It was clear to me during this time that I was to accept that I was the "hired help;" that I was to understand that I worked for the board to be disposed of as they saw fit. On the face of it, this in fact was the case; however, perhaps because I had never treated anyone as "hired help" in my entire life, I found it extremely painful.

Nevertheless, the decision to sideline me was really a blessing for me. I had been fighting too many battles for too long and I was completely worn out from so many years of struggle. And more and more in these last years I had been losing ground in struggles on everything from "academic freedom" to how much money I spent to raise money.

I found the academic freedom battle particularly sad. In our early years, when an adjunct faculty member had repeatedly used the N-word in his class, I had fired him with the full support of the trustees.

In 2009, there had been a new incident in which a faculty member had asked a 62-year-old African-American woman to read a passage from *The Adventures of Huckleberry Finn* that included the N-word several times. The woman had said that it was a word that had caused her a lot of pain in her life and she would prefer not to read it aloud. The teacher said that she would read it herself and the student could leave the room if she wasn't comfortable hearing it.

The student spoke to the vice president of academic affairs about her concern, and he asked the teacher to have a conversation with the student to help the student see that the teacher had not meant to be offensive.

I got an irate call from a trustee to whom the teacher had complained about the vice president's request. The trustee wanted me to countermand him. She saw this concern as "an infringement on academic freedom."

I saw it as insensitivity to the legitimate feelings of the student. In the ensuing half hour conversation in which I steadfastly refused to accede to the trustee's demand, I realized that there was no way to reconcile our points of view.

In the area of fundraising, there were numerous ways in which I had displeased some of the trustees over the years, including serving what they believed to be too much food at board meetings or spending too much money on travel and hotel rooms.

In the twenty years between 1989, when we had our first capital campaign and 2009, I had raised $64 million for a college with no wealthy alumni, the typical source of funds for a college. Raising that much money had involved a lot of travel, a lot of entertaining, and a lot of hotel rooms. These expenses had all been documented and approved by the various trustees who had chaired the board.

But over the years, the trustees who were critical of me always focused on the fundraising activities that didn't result in major gifts. Unfortunately this is a reality of fundraising. As Elizabeth McCormack had said many years ago, fundraising is an art, not a science. And it is a marathon of cultivation and stewardship, not a linear quantifiable process from a request to a gift.

At this time, however, the carping about my performance became a constant topic of discussion. Although no one ever raised any concerns with me directly, the issue of expenses became central to the whispering campaign about me.

It became clear that if I stayed at the college in any capacity once the new president was installed, I would drive myself, as well as everyone else around me, crazy. Nevertheless, this was extraordinarily difficult for me to accept.

Elizabeth McCormack advised me to travel for the six months because she felt that "there was nothing but more heartache ahead." She was right, of course, but I didn't travel. I just tried very hard every single day not to be heartbroken and bitter. I had come to the conclusion early on in this sad chapter that my choices were either to let it go or to have a breakdown. I really didn't want to be institutionalized so I had to find ways to help myself let it go.

Some things were harder than others. One of the aspects of the college in which I took the most pride was the true diversity of the faculty and staff, not only in race and gender but also in socioeconomic background.

Some of the most valuable members of our community were people who had come to the college as entry-level staff, completed their degrees at the college and then gotten promoted into professional positions. This was particularly true in the areas of recruitment, student affairs, and fundraising. These staff members were uniquely equipped to help others see the value of the college through the example of their own lives. They were among our most successful recruiters and fundraisers.

The new president whom the board appointed stopped this benefit of the availability of course work to the staff and also fired many of the community-based staff. When I heard that one of the trustees was boasting that they had gotten rid of all the "unprofessional people," I was devastated.

During the two years that the new president stayed at the college, I felt that all the people whom I had struggled against all of my life had won in the end; as Joan Didion wrote in *The White Album*, "I began to doubt the premise of all the stories I had ever told myself."

But during this same time, I was also approached constantly by people who had a colleague, an employee, a boss, a mother, a son, or a neighbor who was attending Cambridge College.

Every time I met such a person, I would take a deep breath and say, "What kind of an experience is the student having?"

Invariably the answer was some version of "wonderful." The student loves the college, the faculty, and staff. The person had gotten a promotion or new job or a new life.

Although it took almost two years for that president to leave, the mission and the learning model were maintained throughout. The commitment of the faculty and staff and the quality of the students had ensured that the learning continued.

During the years that I taught in Philadelphia, there had been a popular song, "New World Coming," with the lyrics,

> *There's a new world coming*
> *And it's just around the bend*
> *There's a new world coming*
> *This one's coming to an end.*

It was the sentiment of the sixties, and I believed it. I used to quote these lyrics to my students:

> *There's a new day dawning*
> *That belongs to you and me*

Yes a new world is coming
The one we've had visions of
Coming in peace, coming in joy,
Coming in love.

It is hard to believe now that I was ever that hopeful, that naïve, that young. However despite the tremendous struggles, victories were won. Civil rights legislation was passed. Change seemed to be coming across the society.

I was watching television with a group of parents and students from the John Bartram High School when Lyndon Johnson signed the Voting Rights Act of 1965. When President Johnson said "And we shall overcome," that sentence passed through the room like a thunderbolt. Several of the parents started to cry. It was an indescribable moment. Johnson made the hopeful declaration with such conviction. It was so clear that he believed it and so did I. More importantly, President Johnson had convinced a recalcitrant Congress to believe it and to pass the legislation necessary to make it happen.

There has been so much resistance in the years since the legislation was passed, so many attempts to limit it or overturn. But a profound change had been made and its impact has traveled down the generations. As a country, we are not where we had hoped, but we continue to move forward.

I know that my blind belief in possibility allowed me to ignore a lot of reality. And yet, it was the belief that carried me through everything I did. I do believe that that new day is coming but it will require courage and will on the part of the people who work to bring it into being. It's easy to get overwhelmed by what doesn't work, but it is important to build on what does. As Dr. King said during the height of the Civil Rights struggle, "The arc of the universe bends slowly but it bends towards justice."

Over the years I have stayed in touch with many of my former students in Philadelphia. I know a lot of their stories, the ones that had happy endings, students who became doctors and lawyers and college professors and school principals and heads of agencies. And the heartbreaking ones of former students who were killed in the streets, who were in jail or addicted to drugs.

Many individuals linger in my thoughts. Robert Whitt was one of the smartest kids I taught over a fifty-year career; he helped me to understand in my first year of teaching that some wounds can only be healed by affirming action. He broke my pocketbook so that his classmate Ernest could fix it and feel a little bit better about himself. Today, Robert is serving a life sentence in a Pennsylvania prison.

Denny Grasso was a talented musician and songwriter who took a Gerard Manley Hopkins poem that I had taught in class and wrote a beautiful song. He became hopelessly addicted to drugs and died of an overdose.

Then there were the sad stories with happy if ironic endings. Malcolm Bonner was one of the students that the University of Pennsylvania had accepted under protest, and then told that they didn't belong there and worked to get rid of. Malcolm became a heroin addict, went into rehab, came to Cambridge College, graduated and went on to get a doctorate at the Fielding Institute, now the Fielding Graduate University.

He was directing a program at Temple University when he was recruited by the University of Pennsylvania to direct their McNair Scholars Program, designed to help African-American graduate students earn doctorates. Malcolm asked me if I thought he should mention his earlier experiences at Penn.

I said, "Absolutely, perhaps they'll learn something about how they assess potential and support non-mainstream students.

I left Philadelphia because I could no longer be effective after the West Philly student strike and the University of Pennsylvania admissions debacle, but I had also left because I couldn't keep absorbing the pain of watching so many great kids fight so hard against the odds and still lose.

I have gone back to Philadelphia over the years to class reunions and other celebrations and it has helped me to see all the good that

Deborah Jackson, 2019.

came out of those years. There was much more gained than was lost.

I was honored at one of these events and the graduate who introduced me said, "Thank you for seeing so much in us that we didn't see in ourselves."

This sense of "no matter what was lost, so much remains," is even more true about Cambridge College. The students, the faculty, and the staff kept carrying on the mission of the college, despite the turmoil at the top.

After two lost years of failed presidency, the chair of the board at the time, Derek Davis, and others worked hard and successfully to find the right leader for the college.

The good fortune that had always come through for Cambridge College prevailed.

Deborah Jackson, who became president in 2011 is the ideal person. An African-American woman herself, Deborah embraces the college's mission and manifests through her leadership and value system.

Afterword

Cambridge College will surely change as all things change and evolve over time. But as long as many of our academic institutions fail to address societal and learning realities in this 21st Century, there will be a need for our mission.

Cambridge College will always attract students and will survive leadership transitions, enlist supporters, and its mission will thrive.

It will thrive because the need for a Cambridge College is as great today as it was in 1971 when it was founded. The thinking of the teacher from Georgia who in the 1990s reported back to her friends that she "had seen the future" as a student in the college's NITE program was far ahead of the thinking of many leading and acclaimed academic institutions in our country today, which are lagging behind in their responses to the economic, demographic and learning realities of our society.

Colleges and universities today struggle to increase their enrollment of minorities, but how will marginal percentage increases address what is the new face of America in the twenty-first century?

While many educators and administrators in higher education accept the realities of the new demographics of our country—that we are a diverse, multicultural America—most continue to recruit or accept only the top ten percent of all applicants, those who best perform to their standards and practices. This will not address the twenty-first century economic realities of a globalized economy, the kinds of jobs we need to develop in America, and the changing faces, languages and cultural mores of our people. This is the century of the "minority majority," and what used to work no longer will.

Society needs higher education to take the responsibility and provide the leadership to begin to create institutions which are true learning communities. These institutions, set in motion with a moral compass and a social mission, must reflect the strengths and meet the needs of all our citizens. Only educational institutions which themselves incorporate the dynamics of the larger society can aspire to contribute to the recasting of that society. Higher education must send the same structural message as its rhetorical message to reflect through its personnel and its practices a commitment to the diversity that is now America.

To be relevant and to continue to be driving forces within the society as well as the economy, colleges and universities must honor through their faculty and their curriculum the notion that there is no set body of knowledge that each person must acquire and that others will quantify as acceptable (or not); they must accept that each person has things to teach and things to learn, and none of us knows what all of us know.

This is the very heart of the Cambridge College model. Higher education must reflect through its infrastructure and its culture that the ways in which we are the same are so much more powerful than the ways in which we are different, and that the only true aristocracy is that of the human spirit.

Almost seventy years ago, the GI Bill of Rights transformed socioeconomic conditions in America by democratizing higher education. Prior to the enactment of the GI Bill, the nation's colleges and universities were the unquestioned domain of the upper-middle classes.

Discrimination based on race, religion, and gender was commonplace. With the passage of the GI Bill, institutions of higher education were inundated by war veterans. By making higher education accessible to millions, the GI Bill was responsible for the enlargement of the American middle class. Sadly, though, as a result of pressure from Southern Congressmen, the GI Bill was available only to a fraction of the returning Black servicemen.

The GI Bill was signed into law by President Roosevelt, but not without opposition, primarily from within higher education, which feared that the educational component of the bill would be unworkable or that it amounted to a handout for lazy war veterans, most from blue-collar and rural backgrounds. College presidents feared that a sudden influx of war veterans would do irreparable damage to the academic reputations of the nation's institutions of higher education. In fact, the president of the University of Chicago at the time, Robert Maynard Hutchins, worried that campuses would become "educational hobo jungles."

But society prevailed: the gates were thrown open, admission standards were adjusted, and classrooms overflowed with ex-servicemen returned from the war. Higher education would later take great pride in the future accomplishments of these special students and perhaps took credit for their collective acumen, intelligence, grit and determination in transforming the American economy into a powerhouse force in the global market.

In their profiles as older, wiser and more focused applicants to higher education—and especially in their triumphs over adversity, whether personal or in war returning soldiers from WWII are much like the students at Cambridge College. Such students require a different model of learning, as they bring more to the classroom than the typical 18-year-old high school graduate.

One of the more interesting statistics about the GI Bill in the 1940s is that by 1947, it is estimated that 49 percent of students in American colleges and universities were ex-servicemen and women on the GI Bill—nearly all from the working-class of inner cities and rural communities. In all likelihood, they never would have attended college without government financial assistance and its intervention with higher education.

Historians might suggest that government was motivated to underwrite education (and homeownership) for returning servicemen simply to sustain and build a workforce that would grow the economy. Many say today that it is time for government to fashion a new GI

Bill-type of education and housing initiative to revive America in this new world economy by increasing the potential of its new multicultural workforce through investment in education. Certainly the jobs leaving America for countries with lower labor costs must be replaced by the kinds of technology, management and other white-collar jobs that will only develop through an educated workforce.

But the single most important revelation of the GI Bill, one that has application today and always, is that those once not even considered eligible for college in fact excelled and went on to become "The Greatest Generation." This is something for higher education to consider as it evaluates applicants into its fold.

In order to be the true learning communities that the post-industrial age requires, institutions of higher education will have to learn how to become self-reflective and self-renewing. While we will always need centers of advanced scholarship, professional schools of distinction, and even elite, academically superior environments for gifted or lucky young adults, shaping an entire system around these models is the height of economic inefficiency and social irrelevance.

Underlying these suggestions is the notion that every institution in our society must become a true learning community, and colleges and universities are no exception. In fact, the great irony today may be that precisely the institution whose mission is learning may be less of a learning community in twenty-first century terms than many other institutions, including many of our corporations, service agencies, and cultural enterprises.

Colleges must scramble to catch up. This is not something that can be accomplished superficially through an extra course or tutorial. It will require a profound re-examination of the historical evaluation of higher education in America, of the components of the basic mission of our colleges, of the most fundamental structural assumptions which shape curriculum, assessment, and degree-granting, and of the function and role of faculty.

To become once again the true leaders for growth and change they were originally intended to be, colleges will have to look like

America in all its diversity and to function as an institution more in accord with the minds of ordinary people and groups in all their differences of intelligence and spirit. In short, colleges must strive to become once again true learning communities.

Colleges cannot hope to produce such people with the level of consistency and excellence they profess in every other area of their mission unless they themselves restructure. This is the task of a new generation—a new generation unlike those ever seen by higher education, perhaps one capable of changing or creating educational institutions in their likeness, ones like Cambridge College that serve the needs of all students in this minority-majority century.

The challenge isn't whether Cambridge College will survive—it will. The true challenge is whether higher education will change—because it must.

Cambridge College: 50 Years

July 1971. The Institute of Open Education (IOE) begins offering a master's program with 100 students. Tuition: $2,500 annually. Annual budget: $250,000.

July 1973. Newton College closes and IOE affiliates with Antioch College.

1974–1981. Today many of the innovations that IOE Antioch College and Cambridge College introduced are commonplace but in the last quarter of the 20th century, we were one of the few places serving non-traditional students with a distinctive learning model. As a result. Joan Goldsmith and I were asked to consult with a variety of institutions that required innovative approaches to higher education.

IOE Antioch opens its first satellite campus in Springfield, Massachusetts, to work with Browndale, an organization with an international network of group homes for troubled children.

Beginning in 1976, IOE Antioch provided master's programs for Browndale counselors in Toronto, Ontario and Nijmegen, The Netherlands.

1976–1979. In 1976, Joan Goldsmith and I were asked by the Ford Foundation to work with a group of educators in the Bahamas to start a college. Prior to 1975, only 20% of the Bahamian population finished high school and there was no college on the island. Students had to go to the West Indies, Canada, or the United States. Starting in 1975, they took a local high school and turned it into a college.

The most challenging issue was creating a "transitional" education program for people who had never gone to high school to be prepared for entry into college. Many of these prospective students were adults working in managerial positions in the hotel industry, in the casinos and in the banks.

In 1976, we created a transitional education program that assessed the students' learning starting points, designed a program that helped them fill in the gaps in their mastery of high school level work. When the students reached high school level, they were automatically admitted to the College of the Bahamas.

1986–1988. Higher education in Cuba was designed in a very traditional European academic model that culminated in a doctoral degree. There was no curriculum for the preparation of adults for professional positions. Through Peggy Dulany's friendship with Oscar Oramas, the Cuban U.N. Ambassador, I was asked to present a paper on the Cambridge College learning model to a Third World Educational Conference in Havana, Cuba, in 1986. As a result, over the next three years, we put together a team of academics and designed a master's program for colleges in Cuba to prepare managers for Cuba's enterprises.

(Front row) Joan Goldsmith, me, Peggy Dulany, and Linda Goelz with the faculty and students in the program to prepare managers for Cuba's enterprises.

1981. Cambridge College begins as a fully accredited degree granting institution.

1990. The National Institute for Teaching Excellence is established to support practicing teachers who want to complete their master's degree through an intensive summer program and at-a-distance learning in their home school districts during the academic year.

1991. The Masters of Management program was established.

1994. The B.A. program was established. Cambridge College purchased its building at 1000 Massachusetts Avenue, Cambridge.

2021. In addition to its B.A. and master's programs, Cambridge College has a doctoral program and an at-a-distance program, Cambridge College Global Online.

Cambridge College has an annual budget of $39.5 million and 38,000 alumni.

Acknowledgements

To Ann Peretz, who insisted that I finish this book and then helped me to make it happen.

To Jonathan Larsen, who was with me every step of the way.

To Joan Goldsmith, who helped make the dream of Cambridge College a reality.

To Peggy Dulany, whose commitment to social justice made her the ideal partner for me in raising the money necessary to make Cambridge College possible.

To Linda Goelz, who worked her magic behind the scenes to help me accomplish so many things.

To Geraldine Holland, Rosemary Drinka, and Cheryl Bowe, who assisted in the production of the manuscript.

To Bailey Georges, who helped make the final version possible.

To the TidePool Press team, Jock and Frank Herron, Ingrid Mach, and Linda Chadwick, who helped me see this book through to the end.

And, to Conor and Kaitlyn Holland Ruane, who brought me so much joy while I was writing it.